Al Hampel joined B&B in 1969 as executive vice-president in charge of creative services, with a mandate to upgrade the agency's creative image. After the dust had settled, he put down his creative philosophy in a series of house ads. "It's Not Creative Unless It Sells" went on buttons, T-shirts, matchbook covers and framed samplers hand-embroidered by Filipino women.

It's not creative unless it sells.

If anything came out of the so-called creative revolution of the 60's and the recessions of the early 70's, it was a clearer understanding of what advertising is and what it isn't.

By the time those years were over, many advertisers and their agencies had been painfully reminded that advertising was not an art form but a serious business tool. And that "creative advertising" really was advertising that created sales and not just attention.

You might say creativity grew up in those years. And one would think that the mistakes made then would never again be repeated.

Yet here we are, a short time later, and like war and politics, advertising seems to be repeating itself. You need only look at television or pick up a magazine to see the frivolities and ambiguities are passing as creative selling.

It seems such a pity that many advertisers are learning the hard way what some of us have always known.

Not an entertainment medium.

During those crazy 60's, the audience of television rubbed off on the advertising message and more and more advertising tried to become as entertaining as the programming in which it appeared. Very often at the expense of the selling idea. We can still see a rash of imitative commercials following the advent of popular movies, TV programs and feature films. Extravagant commercials featuring everything but a consumer benefit are prevalent. Movie stars and athletes are being used as substitutes for selling ideas.

Awards for what.

Awards for creativity conferred on commercials by advertising people often have nothing to do with advertising that sells. Certainly, nothing to do with the importance of advertising awards has diminished. Their value seems to have depreciated in direct proportion to the proliferation of festivals. In recent times, many began to question the value of being destroyed out of context of sales results.

But as long as advertising awards are written by people, people will continue to win other awards. And that isn't all bad. As Al Jolson once said of Al Jolson, "It's a way to make him happy. You pat him on the back, applaud wildly for lunch, and give a standing ovation for dinner."

You don't have to be loved.

Criticism of an advertising message has little bearing on selling effectiveness. There are many examples of advertising which are disliked by people who react to it to the point of buying.

By the same token, much advertising that is beloved by the critics and consumers alike fizzles badly.

This is not to suggest that advertising need be grating or irritating or hated to be effective. Wouldn't it be great if we could always write advertising that would win awards, that people would love and talk about, and that would sell the product, too?

But, alas, this magic combination is very elusive. And remember, the main objective is not to win awards, not to get people to love your advertising, but to get them to act upon it. In the process of meeting that objective, you may not endear yourself to some consumers but you may become very popular with your stockholders.

Watch out for distraction.

A selling idea runs a very real risk of being swamped by its execution. It's a cliché of the advertising business, but how many times does someone describe a commercial to you almost verbatim and then fail to remember the product? Humor is most often involved. A good joke, a funny piece of action, a great punch line—all can undermine the strongest selling idea. And yet humor, judiciously used, can uplift a piece of advertising, increasing its chances of being remembered while actually enhancing the selling idea. A good test: Is the humor relevant to the message?

Explore the alternatives.

There is no sure way to sell anything. There are many ways to approach the sale of a product—strategically and executionally. Some ways are better than others and you really don't know for sure which is best until you copy test and market test.

The time is long past when an ad agency can deliver a single advertising campaign to a client without examining and presenting alternatives. Every client has the right to take part in the selection process that an agency goes through in leading up to a creative recommendation.

And the most creative campaign is the one that ultimately proves itself in the market.

Don't overshoot the audience.

A lot of words have been written and spoken about advertising catering to the lowest intelligence level of its prospects. That of course is as untrue as it would be unwise.

But equally ridiculous is advertising that wafts over the head of the prospect. We still see and hear commercials and ads that are so cleverly obtuse that they reflect no more than the private narrow world of their creators. For every potential customer who reacts to such "sophisticated" advertising, there are countless others who just don't get it.

There is no "soft sell."

The one factor that did more to end the creative revolution and topple the "creative crazies" from power was the recession of 1970. It was a very sobering experience for many high-flying businesses and advertising agencies.

Creative philosophies seemed to change overnight. "These are hard times that call for hard sell" became the watchword.

But the truth of the matter is: All times are hard times and all times call for hard sell. Hard sell meaning the presentation of a cogent, persuasive idea, stripped of any distracting or irrelevant elements, that will convince people to buy a product. Is there any other kind?

There can be no doubt that advertising today must be more intrusive, more imaginative, more innovative than it has ever been. In a business riddled with sameness and clutter, there is a great virtue in being "creative."

Yet, if ever a word was subject to misinterpretation and confusion, it is the word "creative."

To some it means advertising that wins awards. And there are those who think to be creative, advertising must be talked about at cocktail parties and joked about by comedians.

But "creative" can also mean dramatically showing how a product fulfills a consumer need or desire. Or it can be something as simple as casting the appropriate person for a brand. A unique demonstration of product superiority can be creative. So, of course, can a memorable jingle.

There are probably as many opinions of what is creative as there are people who conceive and judge advertising.

But no matter what your interpretation of the word, one thing is irrefutable:

It's not creative unless it sells.

That, in six words, is the philosophy that guides Benton & Bowles.

If you're a major advertiser in need of truly creative advertising, please call or write to Jack Bowen, President, Benton & Bowles, Inc., 909 Third Avenue, New York, New York 10022. (212) 758-6200.

In the first part of this warm and funny memoir Al Hampel relates his life growing up a poor kid in the industrial city of Paterson, New Jersey.

He attends the Y camp in nearby Pennsylvania as a charity case wearing hand-me-down donations with labels featuring assorted names he never heard of. Just the beginning of his identity crisis he writes.

After high school with WWII in full swing he enlists in the Navy and serves on a repair ship in the Pacific. With benefits from the GI bill Hampel earns a degree in marketing from NYU.

Following a series of small time copywriting jobs, Al lands a position in Young&Rubicam, an ad agency he could only dream of joining . Y&R was considered the most creative of all the shops on Madison Avenue.

He recounts his rise through the ranks, stepping around and over the very talented copywriters who wrote the award winning advertising that set Y&R apart. Along the way he describes the ads and the work habits that helped him scale the Everest of copy departments to become copy chief.

Hampel was a pioneer in the writing of cast or integrated commercials. He would get the scripts of the most popular TV shows weeks in advance and write a minute second ending tailored to the story line of the entire episode. The second ending contained the sponsor's commercial. Viewers believed they were seeing a continuation of the show they were watching but instead they were exposed to a commercial seamlessly and entertainingly. Shows that Hampel wrote second endings for included, Jack Benny, Danny Thomas, Andy Griffith, Hogan's Heroes, Lucy, Gomer Pyle, Jean Arthur, and Laugh In. In those years Hampel wrote the endings to more TV shows than any other writer for television.

In the course of working on the Lay's Potato Chip account Al chose Buddy Hackett to replace Bert Lahr who had been the beloved Lay's spokesman before passing away. It was not an easy transition, but Al formed a close and mutually respectful relationship with Hackett that led to the creation of dozens of humorous spots and a profitable alliance for Frito Lay. In some of the funniest anecdotes in the book Hampel tells of his travels with Buddy, the Vegas years and the celebrities he meets along the way. One chapter describes, "How Buddy Hackett became the Lay's Potato Chip spokesman and how he blew the job."

In the 1970's, Al Hampel wrote one line that he will ever be remembered for and that is now quoted in ad agencies the world over, "It's Not Creative Unless It Sells." Recently he updated the line in keeping with the surge of Internet advertising. "From hits and views you can tell . . . everything but will it sell."

Sticking My Ads Out

It's not creative unless it sells

AL HAMPEL

Copyright © 2012 by Al Hampel.

Library of Congress Control Number:		2012902145
ISBN:	Hardcover	978-1-4691-6284-3
	Softcover	978-1-4691-6283-6
	Ebook	978-1-4691-6285-0

All rights reserved. No part of this book may be reproduced or transmitted in any form or by any means, electronic or mechanical, including photocopying, recording, or by any information storage and retrieval system, without permission in writing from the copyright owner.

This book was printed in the United States of America.

To order additional copies of this book, contact:
Xlibris Corporation
1-888-795-4274
www.Xlibris.com
Orders@Xlibris.com
107369

DEDICATION

This book is dedicated to Dorothy Hampel,
Larry Hampel, Jeffrey Hampel, Julie Roddy, Ian Roddy,
Erin Roddy and Bennett Hampel

CONTENTS

Introduction: It's not creative unless it sells 1
PART 1 Spongecake Ransom 7
PART 2 Call of the Corner 16
PART 3 My Fifteen Minutes 18
PART 4 Alvin to *Zeyde* 21
PART 5 Boot Camp for the Imagination 25
PART 6 World War and Other Conflicts 29
PART 7 Civvies to Skivvies 32
PART 8 A Sailor's Life for Me 36
PART 9 How I Helped Win the War 39
PART 10 The Ascent Begins 41
PART 11 Tuxedo Junction 44
PART 12 Swept Off My Feet 46
PART 13 Discouraged but Undeterred 48
PART 14 Last Stop Before New York 50
PART 15 A New York Job with a Lifetime Benefit 52
PART 16 Hangin' with Kong 55
PART 17 Is This a Joke? 58
PART 18 And Then I Wrote 61
PART 19 An Auspicious Beginning 65
PART 20 As If It Was Yesterday 67
PART 21 No Buddy Can Eat Just One 69
PART 22 People Who Never Thought They'd Meet Al Hampel 73
PART 23 Countdown to Liftoff 75
PART 24 Among My Souvenirs 79
PART 25 The Carol Channing Show 82
PART 26 The Speech 85

INTRODUCTION

IT'S NOT CREATIVE UNLESS IT SELLS.

If anything came out of the so-called creative revolution of the 60's and the recession of 1970, it was a clearer understanding of what advertising is and what it isn't.

By the time that era was over, many advertisers and their agencies had been painfully reminded that advertising was not an art form but a serious business tool. And that "creative advertising" really was advertising that created sales and not just attention.

You might say creativity grew up in those years. And one would think that the mistakes made then would never again be repeated.

Yet here we are, a scant half-dozen years later, and like war and politics, advertising seems to be repeating itself. You need only look at television or pick up a magazine to se the frivolities and ambiguities that are passing as creative selling.

Once again many advertisers are learning-the hard way—what some of us have always known:

NOT AN ENTERTAINMENT MEDIUM.

During those crazy 60's, the ambience of television rubbed off on the advertising message and more and more advertising tried to become as entertaining as the programming in which it appeared—very often at the expense of the selling idea. One can still see a plethora of imitative commercials following the advent of popular new television programs and feature films. Remember all those "Bonnie and Clyde" commercials or the dozen of "Yellow Submarine" animated spots that followed that feature film? And how about the recent rash of "Gatsby" takeoffs?

AWARDS OF WHAT.

Awards for creativity conferred by juries of advertising people often have nothing to do with advertising that sells. Certainly, in recent years, the importance of advertising awards has diminished. Their value seems to have decreased in direct proportion to the proliferation of festivals. At the same time, many began to question the worth of honors bestowed out of context of sales results.

But as long as advertising will continue to be written by people, people will continue to give each other awards. And that isn't all bad. George Burns once said of Al Jolson, "It was easy enough to make him happy. You just had to cheer him for breakfast, applaud wildly for lunch, and give him a standing ovation for dinner."

YOU DON'T HAVE TO BE LOVED.

Criticism of an advertising campaign has little bearing on selling effectiveness. There are many examples of advertising which are disliked by the very people who are reacting to the message.

By the same token, much advertising that is beloved by the critics and consumers alike fizzle badly.

This is not to suggest that advertising need be grating or irritating or hated to be effective. Wouldn't it be great if we could always write advertising that would win awards, that people would love and talk about, and that would sell the product, too?

But, alas, this magic combination is very elusive. And remember, the main objective is not to win awards, not to get people to love your advertising, but to get them to act upon it. In the process of meeting that objective, you may not endear yourself to some consumers but you may become very popular with your stockholders.

WATCH OUT FOR DISTRACTION.

A selling idea runs a very real risk of being swamped by its execution. It's a cliché of the advertising business, but how many times does someone describe a commercial to you almost verbatim and then fail to remember the product? Humor is most often involved. A good joke, a funny piece of action, a great punch line—all can undermine that strongest selling idea. And yet humor, judiciously used, can uplift a piece of advertising, increasing its chances of being remembered while actually enhancing the selling idea. A good test: Is the humor relevant to the message?

EXPLORE THE ALTERNATIVES.

There is no sure way to sell anything. There are many ways to approach the sale of a product—strategically and executionally. Some ways are better than others and you really don't know for sure which is best until you copy test and market test.

The time is long past when an ad agency can deliver a single advertising campaign to a client without examining and presenting alternatives. Every client has the right to take part in the selection process that an agency goes through in leading up to a creative recommendation.

And the most creative campaign is the one that ultimately proves itself in the market.

DON'T OVERSHOOT THE AUDIENCE.

A lot of words have been written and spoken about advertising catering to the lowest intelligence level of its prospects. That of course is an untrue as it would be unwise.

But equally ridiculous is advertising that wafts over the head of the prospect. We still see and hear commercials and ads that are so cleverly obtuse that they reflect no more than the private narrow world of their creators. For every potential customer who reacts to such "sophisticated" advertising, there are countless others who just don't get it.

THERE IS NO "SOFT SELL".

The one factor that did more to end the creative revolution and topple the "creative crazies" from power was the recession of 1970. It was a very sobering experience for many high-flying businesses and advertising agencies.

Creative philosophies seemed to change overnight. "These are hard times that call for hard sell" became the watchword.

But the truth of the matter is: All times are hard times and all times call for hard sell. Hard sell meaning the presentation of a cogent, persuasive idea, stripped of any distracting or irrelevant elements, that will convince people to buy a product. Is there any other kind?

There can be no doubt that advertising today must be more intrusive, more imaginative, more innovative than it has ever been. In a business riddled with sameness and clutter, there is a great virtue in being "creative".

Yet, if ever a word was subject to misinterpretation and confusion, it is the word "creative".

To some it means advertising that wins awards. To others it is advertising that makes people laugh. And there are those who think to be creative, advertising must be talked about at cocktail parties and joked about by comedians.

But "creative" can also mean dramatically showing how a product fulfills a consumer need or desire. Or it can be something as simple as casting the appropriate person for a brand. A unique demonstration of product superiority can be creative. So, of course, can a memorable jingle.

There are probably as many opinions of what is creative as there are people who conceive and judge advertising.

But no matter what your interpretation of the word, one thing is irrefutable.

IT'S NOT CREATIVE UNLESS IT SELLS.

I am including the enclosed ad that I wrote as an introduction to this book because it contains my philosophy of advertising. The ad appeared in Fortune in 1974 and other periodicals and became the cornerstone of a campaign for the advertising agency, Benton&Bowles for which I served as creative director.

PART 1

Spongecake Ransom

GOT SILK? IF you were around in the 1930s or '40s and answered yes, there's a good chance that your silk came from the looms of H&H Silk Co. on Matlock Street, in a grimy section of the mill town of Paterson, New Jersey. Paterson was my hometown and known the world over as the Silk City. One of the *H*s was Leo Hampel, my father, who tended to his six looms like a rancher to his flock. Weaving was the skill my father brought with him from the Polish textile hub of Lodz, so it was no surprise that upon arriving in America, he teamed with his brother Isadore and bought a half-dozen looms from Crompton & Knowles on credit, a lot of credit.

I must have been about seven or eight when, as a treat, my dad took me to the shop. In my family, it was always the shop, never the mill or the factory. On first confronting a loom, I remember stepping back from the monster, a complex machine about the size of an armored personnel carrier and looking just as warlike. Parts were interacting every which way, shuttles east and west, reeds north and south, plus quills and bobbins and warps. All working in tandem and creating a din that jarred the teeth and buckled the floor. Oil and grease stains served as floor coverings. This was the way my father earned a living every day, six days a week, and many hours of overtime in that dirt and noise. No wonder he shouted when he talked. But from this cacophony and drudgery came lustrous, slinky, sexy silk, prized by fashionistas far and wide. I knew then and there, this was not how I wanted to spend my life. The language of our house was Yiddish. So I spoke Yiddish before I spoke English. When my parents didn't want me to hear something, they spoke to each other in a very broken English. Both immigrants from Poland, they were in America longer than I was.

My father's skills really came to the fore whenever there was a "smetsh," Leo Hampel's word for smash, a monumental screwup that came with the ominous grinding of metal and a halt to weaving followed by silence as if the machine needed to take a break. A smash was costly as production stopped, and the output of silk diminished. On his knees or on his back, Dad had little time to find the cause of the breakdown and fix it. Loom fixers were a special breed with intimate knowledge of every inch of the loom and how to get the beast working again. My dad was an ace loom fixer, and later in life, he applied his skills in other shops.

The specialty of H&H Silk Co. was tie silk, the very finest of the breed that became the costly cravats that adorned the necklines of gentlemen who could afford the finest. There was no room for error in the manufacture of tie silk. Nary a slub was acceptable. Any misweave voided that day's production. Money down the drain. I like to think that H&H silk went into the making of the luxury ties that a short salesman named Ralph Lifshitz was selling to fine stores everywhere. Ralph Lifshitz went on to become Ralph Lauren. Leo Hampel went on to become bankrupt. Alas, the textile industry began to abandon Paterson, New Jersey, for more profitable climes in the South, where labor was cheaper and unions nonexistent. Caught in that squeeze, H&H was forced to sell its looms for scrap. And many times I thought those mashed, chopped-up H&H looms came back to haunt America via Tokyo and Iwo Jima. Ironically, much of the world's raw silk came from the silkworms of Japan.

At home, Mary, my mother, cooked and baked, cleaned, and washed clothes by hand and hung them on the line to dry. No one cooked and baked or cleaned like Mary. Oh, how I lust today for that home cooking and specially baked goods that I didn't appreciate as a kid. Gefilte fish, matzo balls, potato balls vegetable soup, stuffed cabbage, stuffed veal, stuffed derma, and stuffed family and friends around the dinner table. All cooking done without referring to a recipe and never anything written down. What happens in Mary's kitchen stays in Mary's kitchen. But what Mom did best was importune for her kids, my brother Dan and me, to excel in school. This we did without fail lest as she would say, "You'll wind up working in your father's shop." If any mother was the driving force behind her kid's success, Mary would be at the wheel of a stretch Rolls-Royce. My brother went on to a hugely successful career as an electrical engineer. Me? Well,

I went into advertising. Once when I came home without a gold star on my report card, my mother asked, "What happened to the honor roll this term?"

"I didn't like the teacher very much."
"Why not?"
"She came to my desk and told me that Palmer was probably spinning in his grave and my handwriting was better left in the inkwell. When she leaned down, she had bad breath. She eats ham sandwiches."

After Dad's business failed, household income dwindled. We were also in the last stages of a depression, so like most families in our neighborhood, we made some adjustments to maintain some semblance of our comfortable lifestyle. Dad picked up temporary jobs as a loom fixer in assorted mills. At one point, my mother took a job as a quill winder, a less labor-intensive task in the weaving process, one more suitable for a woman. But one day, an errant shuttle, which had become a dangerous flying missile, hit her ear and impaired her hearing ever since. Despite the cutbacks, we continued to live at 348 East Twenty-Third Street, in a wooden frame, four-story house and never missed a rent payment. Dad shoveled coal, kept the fire alive, and hauled ashes to keep our flat warm and have hot water during the winter. I shared one of our two bedrooms with my brother.

The apartment was located over Freed's grocery store, which was very convenient since we had an arrangement with Mr. Freed to buy groceries without cash. Freed recorded our purchases in a ledger, and at the end of the month, we would pay up. I was never sure about Freed's bookkeeping or arithmetic, but we enjoyed mutual trust. I wasn't aware of it at the time, but we were living a sort of generic existence. My parents, especially my mother, slaved to maintain our standard of living. She was so good at keeping us afloat in the style to which we were accustomed that I can't say I was deprived. I would never have described us as poor. We were just very, very not well-off. Nevertheless, the signs of poverty were clear and omnipresent. We had no car, so we relied on the Madison Avenue bus to take us downtown and back. The fare was ten cents for a half-hour ride with lots of stops along the way. Once in a while, our generous neighbor, Mr. Resnick, invited us for a ride around the environs of Paterson in his vintage Packard. Oh, how I looked forward to this treat to glimpse a bit of the world outside my small circle.

The only phone in the building was in Freed's, so we were permitted to make and receive emergency calls on Freed's phone. I had no bike and no sled to enjoy the steep Eighth Avenue hill in winter. One January day, when the snow was packed tight, even icy, a friend let me use his sled. It was the loan that came close to ending my life at an early stage. As I reached the bottom of the hill at an incredible speed, a car made a turn right into my path. I steered to avoid a collision but not enough to avoid ramming into the right rear tire of the oncoming car. Thrown from the sled and deposited in a snowbank at the side of the road, the car stopped, and out came the driver, a woman who had heard a jolt and looking as though she had just run over and killed a kid with her car. There I was immobilized—not by the snow, but by terror, terror of what might have been and how I would have to explain it to my mother.

During this embargo on what little luxuries we might have enjoyed, there were still ways a kid could pass the time enjoyably even if in the imagination. I would invent games and actually execute some of them out of available cardboard and a pair of dice. Football and baseball with teams drawn up from box scores in the daily news provided many hours of fun with or without a friend to play with. I announced these games as though I was on radio fancying myself as Mel Allen or Red Barber. I created a game of chance constructed on a wooden crate with a circle of seven numbers and a spinner in the middle. A poor man's roulette. With a meager allowance, I bought a small board game called Kentucky Derby on which you moved your horse one space at a time according to where the spinner landed. The horses were named War Admiral, Twenty Grand, Omaha, Gallant Fox, Cavalcade, and other great racehorses of the time. Of course, I described the races as any good announcer would. While the country was caught up in Monopoly mania, my friends and I made do with a pale and cheaper imitation called Big Business. None of us could afford the real thing. There was never a shortage of food during this time of need.

Our family was eventually forced to enroll in a poverty program sponsored by the City of Paterson. It was called being on relief, and it consisted mainly of food stamps. My mother hated this dole, but she swallowed her pride to keep her family in calories. I remember one Thanksgiving, a big truck came through the neighborhood, delivering the equivalent of CARE packages to those "on relief." I was so embarrassed I ignored the delivery man seeking out our apartment to make the ignominious drop. Yet the special Thanksgiving package found its way to our door. We were the recipients of a turkey and all the trimmings. My mom sorted through the goody bag, keeping the pareve items, but disposing the turkey, lard, and other nonkosher items. Our Thanksgiving was more of a kosher chicken and schmaltz event. Aunt Selma, my mother's older sister, came to America several years before the rest of the family. In her mind, this endowed her with a sense of superiority, which characterized her demeanor ever since. She shed, she thought, all semblance of her roots and spoke only English. But it was English with a pretty heavy Yiddish accent, although everyone kept it hidden from her so she really considered herself a *Yenkee*—a grand dame who always knew more about all things than anyone else. "Mary," she would say to my mother, "you need to take Elvin [for Alvin] to a doctor, he's too skinny. I can see his heart beating in his chest. That's not right. You let him join the Cub Scouts? Oh no, they take the Boy Scouts first when there is a war."

Once when I spilled my chocolate milk, she wiped up the mess with a washcloth, then squeezed the contents back into my glass. Since I was away from home and a five-year-old guest at Aunt Selma's summer rental in Goshen, New York, I thought I better do what I was told, so I drank it.

Aunt Selma's only child was Florence, the wunderkind, best in everything she tried. She also was, hands down, the best spoiled brat in all of Bensonhurst, where the Waxmans chose to settle as immigrants. Uncle Nathan was a kindly old soul who worked as a furrier and served as a living ATM for Florence. Aunt Selma ran a sewing machine at a dress factory close to home. Friends at work were always giving Aunt Selma gifts, some of which she tried to pawn off on us. In a closet in the Waxman apartment, there was a bag filled with brand-new, tags still on, merchandise. Most of it was assorted items of clothing. None of this loot was ever appropriate for my family, but one time, Selma insisted I take and wear a brand-new pair of blue suede shoes. "You look good in them." My new blue suede shoes were about three sizes too big, but Aunt Selma made sure we took them home because they were beautiful and expensive. So before there was Elvis, there was Elvin and his blue suede shoes. I never wore them. My family and I were convinced that Aunt Selma's friends at work were stationed right where all that stuff fell off the truck. Lest I forget, let me tell you about my flat feet. How flat? It was as though all the air went out of my tires and I was walking on the rims. Some expert on all matters, probably

Aunt Selma, strongly advised that I should be wearing arch supports. Thus, I was outfitted with clunky metal arch inserts that were so uncomfortable and sharp along the edges they cut through the leather of my ugly high-top shoes. As though the kids in school needed more material for jokes. If I had ever passed through a metal detector with those arches, I would immediately be taken into custody. And the front-page headline in the next day's *New York Post* would read, 8-YEAR-OLD SHOE BOMBER CAUGHT FLAT.

I had fun with cousin Florence and actually enjoyed her craziness, but one time, as we were in the bathtub together, don't ask how that ever came about, but during that infamous scrub down, cousin Florence bit me in the stomach and left the imprint of her teeth on me for months. It's a good thing her aim was not too good or we'd be going to another bris. The main thing I liked about visiting Aunt Selma and Florence was the location of their home, just ten minutes by trolley to my vacation paradise—Coney Island. It wasn't exactly St. Bart's or Barbados, but it didn't have jellyfish or urchins to avoid in the surf. All you had to look out for were used condoms. I could think of no place that would be more fun for an eight-year-old than Coney Island.

After a day at the beach, we had the boardwalk to look forward to. The boardwalk had all the glitter and excitement for kids that Las Vegas held out to adults. On the boardwalk, you had many games of chance in the numerous penny arcades. Payoffs were mainly in free plays. Skee-Ball was a game of skill, and you would accumulate cards redeemable in junk prizes, most of them stuffed. Steeplechase Park was the Taj Mahal of amusements on the boardwalk. The only way I gained entry was via someone's thrown-away ticket that had some unused rides. So one time, I did get to hold on for life and scream in terror on the legendary Cyclone roller coaster. I also rode the famous racehorses and walked the rotating barrel and drove the "bump 'em" cars and saw Coney Island from the huge Ferris wheel. While Coney didn't have the great restaurants of Vegas, it did have the best frozen custard and the one and only Nathan's hot dogs, which were well worth risking the wrath of God for eating *treyf* (nonkosher). I have never eaten hot dogs as fabulous as those. I now salivate at the memory.

At the southern end of the boardwalk was Luna Park, the other assemblage of rides and fascinating freak shows. It was theater to hear the barkers make extravagant claims of the rarities to be seen inside: the sword swallower, the fire eater, the snake charmer, a hermaphrodite, the bearded lady, the world's strongest man, the tattooed wonder, and more. From the fast-talking comedic pitch of the barker, I took my first lesson in writing ad copy. I could never afford a ticket, and I was young for them to sell me one, but just hearing about these wonders of the world triggered all kinds of images, none so vivid as the beautiful Tirza in her amazing bath of wine. Yes, up on the stage was this huge colored poster featuring a gigantic wineglass into which Tirza—"Naked as the day she was born," the barker said—was shown lolling in Bordeaux, legs sexily dangling over the rim. At first, I thought, *This is funny, didn't she turn all purple? Does the ticket include watching her shower afterward?* These were the thoughts of a wide-eyed kid mesmerized by the beautiful Tirza seen only through a deep purple, cheaply silk-screened backdrop, but even then, what started out as funny became a more serious, but pleasant sensation. In my young but fertile mind, I probably saw more of Tirza than the paying audience did. Recently, I received an email from a woman who thanked me for writing nice things about Tirza, she's the one who takes a bath in wine.

"She is my grandmother."

One summer, the YMHA of Paterson sponsored an all-expense-paid two-week stay at a summer camp for kids whose families could not afford to send them. It was sort of a Fresh Air Fund of the day. Naturally my mother enrolled me. "You'll make new friends. You'll play sports. You'll have a good time." She could not have argued more convincingly to get this response: "No way." With the registration form came a list of required camp clothes of which I owned a precious few. Next thing I know, a box arrives through special delivery with more than enough camp gear for two weeks, each piece with an ID label sewn in the shoulder. Names I never heard of. All garments, as they say of used cars, previously owned. "I'm not going," I protested even as I boarded the Lehigh Valley train to Port Jervis, New York, and then on to Milford, Pennsylvania, and Camp Cedar Crest, a picturesque sylvan retreat in the Poconos, my home for the next two weeks. As predicted, I soon adjusted and even began to enjoy camp. Apparently, former wearers of my new identity outfits left some extra-base hits in their T-shirts and some amazing basketball shots in my shorts. They must have been jocks, and for this, I belatedly thank them very much. They not only helped me trade the tar-bubbling pavements of Paterson for a cool and welcome, but all too short, respite in the country. I learned to swim, was elected captain of the basketball team, scored some points in games, and actually hit the softball out of the infield. All of these for a kid whose only previous athletic experience consisted of rooting for the Boston Red Sox. I never suffered the expected identity crisis despite labels to the contrary. In two weeks, I became known as Alvin, that fun kid from Paterson.

Bubbe, my maternal grandmother, often spent time in our flat. When my mother went to work, Bubbe played nanny, babysitter, cook (pasta with ketchup), and wise old storehouse of amusing and often ridiculous *bubbemeises* (myths, superstitions, old wives' tales). Bubbe never did learn English, so from her, I learned Yiddish, many words of which no English translation can accurately do justice. While Bubbe didn't invent the spitless spit, she surely was one of its seasoned practitioners. *Ptooey*. I first heard the sound and saw the gesture whenever the name Hitler was mentioned. She would put her head down and with an emphatic shake would spray *ptooey* meant to curse the ruthless dictator and wishing him in *drayed* (buried). Grandma's only son, Herschel, my uncle, and his family perished in the Holocaust. *Ptooey* was also implied when *treyf* (nonkosher foods) or *chometz* (not kosher for Passover) were mentioned in an effort to ward off the ingestion of such foods. Bubbe would look skyward as if to imply, God is watching. I was so impressed with these incantations that I did not violate the rules until many years later, and even when I did eat something I wasn't supposed to, I believed I was committing a sin and would be punished. I didn't eat bacon, ham, or shellfish until I served in the navy many years later, and to this day, I shun such foods.

Some typical bubbemeises: If you let your fingernails grow long, you will have bad luck. If you eat standing up, the food will go to your legs. The best physic (laxative) is an enema. Eat a flat piece of toast (a *panetzl*) liberally slathered with garlic (*knoble*), and you poison all the germs in your system. The one and only cure for acne is urine. The best cure for digestive problems is a mixture of rhubarb and soda.

Bubbe compounded this remedy at home by combining shavings from a well-aged chunk of rhubarb with baking soda. The results were preserved in jars and looked exactly like jars of mud. It's been written that uncooked rhubarb is about as delectable as pond algae. Those who could stomach this concoction swore it worked.

It was a time of highly publicized kidnappings in the country, headlined by the Lindbergh tragedy. To prevent my being snatched, Bubbe was assigned to get me when school let out, and one day, in the boisterous crowd of parents and schoolkids that milled about at session's end, one woman grabbed my arm and said, "Come to Momma." I do remember the event, and to me, it was simply a case of reaching for the wrong arm. But to her dying day, Bubbe remained convinced that I was about to be kidnapped and that she saved my life. If she was right, it would have been the world's first kidnapping ransomed with all that my family could afford to pay—a homemade sponge cake.

PART 2

Call of the Corner

EVER SINCE DICK and Jane, I do not remember a time when I was not an avid reader. I read everything in print: newspapers, magazines, books, comic books, mailings, ads, signs, cereal boxes, direction inserts, etc. I love words. I once contracted to sell magazines door-to-door, cold calling and hawking *Saturday Evening Post, Liberty, Woman's Home Companion, Colliers*. The payoff was not in money, but in prizes. My first award for selling three dollars worth of magazines was a balsa wood glider, which, on its maiden flight, landed high atop a factory and was never seen again. Not at all bad because between sales, and there was a lot of "between," I could read those magazines. But from the time I was able to borrow books from a branch library near my house, I fell madly in love with books. I became the library's most frequent borrower, two books every two weeks, and never a late return. I had a truly catholic taste, reading such authors as Jack London, Upton Sinclair, John Steinbeck, Zane Grey, James Fenimore Cooper. I enjoyed nonfiction too, particularly books on current events and biographies. I was also hooked on series written for young readers, Bomba the Jungle Boy and the Tom Swift adventures.

But reading, like writing, was a lonely pursuit, so in time, I put my books aside for a while and ventured out of doors, particularly to the corner of Eighth Avenue and Twenty-Third Street, the site of old man Kay's candy store and the gathering place of most of my contemporaries. I slowly acquired the art of hanging out, just hanging out, and doing a lot of nothing but schmoozing and absorbing, a little singing, goofing with one another, arguing over baseball, doing imitations of neighborhood characters, and creating minor mischief like loud noise that drew the ire of old man Kay who threatened to call the cops, which he never did. The corner was also the arena for a bunch of small ball games, played with that old standby, the "spaldeen" (read as Spalding), a pink rubber ball, which could then be purchased for a nickel. There was box ball, wall ball, stoop ball, corner ball, and of course, stick ball. There was no surface exempt from a rendezvous with a "spaldeen." And at times, we were chased for creating a nuisance. The snack du jour at Kay's cost a dime and consisted of a pretzel log and a Pepsi. Pepsi was newly introduced to compete with Coke on a strategy of more for your money: Pepsi Cola hits the spot—twelve full ounces. That's a lot. Twice as much for your money too. Pepsi Cola is the drink for you. Trickle, trickle, trickle. And then back on the street to see who could come up with the loudest burp. The corner proved popular with adults as well as the guys. From a radius of about five blocks, people came to Kay's candy store. They stopped for an ice-cream cone, to buy newspapers and magazines, some even to tilt with the pinball machine or play the numbers. So Kay's became a special salon, a town square serving the enlarged neighborhood where customers could stop for a few minutes after their purchases to chat with the boys, exchange stories, catch up on gossip, or watch us play the corner games, which were always a hoot. We went at it as if we were in the big leagues, and like the big leagues, even more fun when fights broke out. The gang was always good for laughs. Frankie Scaz would regale us with stories from the Spotless Dry Cleaners factory where he had a part-time job: No use standing on the seat, Spotless crabs jump six feet.

It was kind of amazing to me, but more and more adults began to show up at the corner of Eighth Avenue and Twenty-Third Street. A candidate for mayor of Paterson was a regular, as was a doctor, a chief of police, a fireman, a mailman, and a bus driver, assorted businessmen, a circle of grown-ups eager to mix with the guys, exchange anecdotes, and have a few laughs. We attracted a membership of regulars, and while I was not aware of it at the time, I was continuing my education in a way no school or book could deliver. I was working on my degree in street smarts. Of what benefit to men and women their various degrees from prestigious universities if they do not have street smarts? They are among the truly disadvantaged. I was once asked to define street smarts. "Street smart" means never having to be called a schmuck.

PART 3

My Fifteen Minutes

NOT BEING A very high draft pick, when sides were chosen to play stickball, I was in charge of the stick. So it was not unusual in the summer of my twelfth year to find me rummaging through backyards in search of mops and brooms that were near death and would welcome decapitation and mercy killings. When I would show up with a new stick, I was rewarded by calling balls and strikes, should the games involve realistic baseball conditions. Occasionally, I would get to pinch-hit. Thus, I found myself in a no-win situation, being harassed for striking out or maligned for making bad calls. In late August, as the sun was setting on the summer vacation, the recreational office of the city of Paterson, in a move to shift gangs from the streets to the ball fields, created a city softball league. We never considered ourselves members of a gang nor did we have an organized softball team. Nevertheless, we found our neighborhood scheduled to play a team from across the tracks, a section normally off limits to our guys because those kids were said to be hooligans who would pick on stragglers into their territory.

The game was to be played on a Sunday morning at Lafayette oval, their home field. Too embarrassed to call the whole thing off, we hastily put together a ragtag team and called ourselves Amicis. Bull Horowitz, one of our more learned members came up with name. "It's Latin for friends," he told us. Having little time to argue, we went along with a name sure to instill fear into the opposing team, the Eighteenth Street Raiders. The Amicis featured the best jocks that could be assembled from a nice, friendly neighborhood where the worst *shonda* (scandal) was bull walking out of Kay's with a comic book under his coat and the book falling out from under when confronted by old man Kay.

As luck would have it, we were one player short on the day of the game, so they all looked at me, and I became the starting left fielder, a position deemed least risky to the team's success. My palms immediately began to wet the inside of my borrowed fielder's glove. You might say the game was decided when the Raiders showed up. As they jumped from a beat-up pickup, they looked more like members of a work release gang than a softball team. They were a motley crew, but they had beautiful black-and-gold team shirts with names like Tony, Wolf, Angelo, Mario, Spider, Turk, and Rocco who turned out to be their pitcher. Our team featured Marvin, Marty, Seymour, Worm, Harry, Squirrel, Burton, Scaz, Sidney, Stewie, and me, Alvin. However, in my neighborhood, I was known as Ted, as in Ted Williams, my idol. This was a blessing since *Alvin* was then a popular name of a chipmunk. Anyway, if you lined us up, we looked just like a class that had just come home from Temple.

Our first six batters struck out. They called him Rocket because he seemed to have one attached to his arm. We watched as a softball turned into a pea. We soon knew that we were in a laugher. Our Scaz was a pretty good pitcher, but he was not having luck getting anyone out. Third inning, the score 11 to nothing and another long fly ball, this one in the area of left field, where you might remember I was standing. The ball was coming my way, and I was thinking, *Oy vey, Hampel, this is it.* First, I ran in, then I stumbled back, then to the side. The ball seemed to be drifting. Understand, the surface of this outfield made Mars look like a croquet lawn. *With a little luck*, I thought, *I would disappear into one of those craters.* A lot of breaths were held on our sideline. After what seemed like an eternity, that nice and friendly ball found its way into my glove. A huge cheer went up from the spectators.

But it's not over, Hampel. You have to bat. Until my turn, our team had just one feeble groundout. Even though my heart was thumping and my hands were clammy, I believe I made an imposing figure at the plate. From the time they started calling me Ted, I worked on developing a formidable batting stance and a smooth swing of the bat, homage to Ted Williams. I might not get a lot of hits, but I had a beautiful swing. Behind me, their catcher yelled to the Rocket, "Careful, this guy looks like a hitter." I turned and said, "Would you say that louder please?" He did, and suddenly, I'm feeling like the legendary hitter I was named after. I swung at the next pitch and lofted a lazy fly ball into the short left field. The shortstop drifted out; the left fielder came running in. And I'm standing there in a trance hearing, "Run, run, run, what are you standing there for?" Before I could reach first, anyone else would have been on third, the left fielder, running as though he was on fire, made a spectacular shoestring catch. The only member of the Amicis to hit a ball out of the infield, I was greeted as a hero with much applause and high fives. So what if we lost 21-0? So what if Rocket had sixteen strikeouts? So what if our five pitchers gave up a dozen hits and almost as many walks? A miraculous catch—miraculous for me, routine for anyone else—robbed of the only hit we could muster. I reached the acme of my athletic career, my fifteen minutes of fame, even though it came in a losing cause.

PART 4

Alvin to *Zeyde*

ZEYDE IS THE Yiddish word for grandfather, and according to Leo Rosten, *zeyde* is best defined as "the press agent for his grandchildren." So it was Zeyde that took me not just as his favorite grandkid but as a treasured client. My grandfather was known around town as the tall "Mondle" although his name was Louis Mandel. There was another Mandel in Paterson; he was the short red-faced "Mondle." The two were never mixed up, but they were friends and hung out at the Jersey Verein Club on Main Street in Paterson. There the guys played pinochle and had a few schnapps. The club was a cozy wood-paneled suite furnished with card tables and one great pool table on which I was permitted to try my hand while waiting for Grandpa to take me home. The card players would look over at my imitation of a pool hustler and wink and tease Mondle about his kid the shark at the table, all form, no skill. Remember, I was all of eight at the time and had just come off acing a Stanford-Binet test, scoring the IQ of a thirteen-year-old. Grandpa made this result known to all who would listen. And so in my grandfather's inner and outer circle, I was looked upon as some kind of boy genius. Living up to the hype gave me headaches, but in no way would I ever want to disappoint my beloved press agent. Zeyde was a distinguished-looking six footer with wavy silvery gray hair. He was always nattily dressed, and though his suits were not bespoke, his look was impeccable, and his attire gave off-the-rack a good name. In summer, he always wore a boater, not so much to protect from the sun, but to appear fashionable. He delighted in telling me of the time he attended a Yankee game and Babe Ruth hit a home run. In the ensuing excitement, someone tossed his hat on to the field. He was not upset because the thrill of seeing the Babe come through was worth it. I wonder what Zeyde would think if he knew that his favorite *einekle* (grandchild) became a die-hard Boston Red Sox fan.

His class extended even to the cigarettes he smoked—Helmar, an oval-shaped brand of strong Turkish tobacco, which came in an attractive, colorful package that featured a white silhouette of a queen bracketed by stunning graphics of a Middle East origin. The Helmar box is now a collectible and can be purchased on eBay. Zeyde saved the Helmar boxes for me, and I used them for storing stamps, coins, marbles, etc. Kids love boxes and were forever cadging them from grocery stores (cheese boxes were at a premium), candy stores, hardware stores, and crazy Benny was known to hit on the undertaker for empty boxes. To this day, I can hardly separate myself from boxes, and I have stacks of them around the house.

If Zeyde were alive, he'd be right on line for the iPhone. He loved buying the latest audio equipment. He owned a beautiful console Fada radio with a built-in Victrola on which he played opera records and drove my grandmother nuts. He also was the first in his circle to own a car, a machine they called it then. He bought a Hupmobile, rolled it over on a country road, and almost killed his wife and my aunt Anna.

One memorable day, he decided it was time I visited New York City. So off we went to the Erie Railroad station in Paterson, up a flight of stairs to await the main line train headed for New York. With a roar reminiscent of a clap of thunder, that huge steam engine pulling a half-dozen passenger cars created a windstorm, startling and thrilling me at the same time as it pulled into the station. This was not Thomas the Tank Engine. This was the same steamer that hauled the twentieth century to Chicago west. What a beauty. Later in life, I owned a train set that featured a replica of that engine but was powered not by coal but by a huge key that you had to wind and wind until the engine was ready to ride the rails. That set was the poor relative of the famous Lionel electric trains, but it worked, and my thumb grew a lovely callus from winding. Another toy I wish I had kept. The Erie main line ended at the huge busy railroad yard in Jersey City. Dozens of trains disgorging passengers and waste, hissing and sputtering, I never forgot the tumultuous sounds and the noxious smells of that terminal. Now Zeyde and I disembarked and hurried a short distance to catch the ferry, which would take us to Chambers Street and the subway to midtown Manhattan. The ferry ride was my maiden voyage on water, and I've loved to travel by ship ever since. Some years later, 1944, I joined the navy and was a sailor in World War II. First, Zeyde took me to Macy's, the largest department store in the world. Then to the Empire State Building, the world's tallest building. Now for a little lunch at the amazing Automat. Oh, the stories I would relate to my friends in Paterson: There's the one of a new immigrant who went to the Automat on his first day in America where he was seen feeding one nickel after another into the cherry pie slot. "Are you crazy?" his cousin asked him. "You already have a dozen pieces of pie!" The greenhorn replied, "What's it to you if I keep winning?" I settled for one piece of coconut custard pie. But what an amazing place. You put coins in a slot, and out comes food, hot or cold. Who's behind those slots on the wall, the Wizard of Oz? Zeyde could not have taken me to a more entertaining destination.

When I arrived back in Paterson and tried to describe the trip to my non-English-speaking bubbe, I told her of seeing *yahmen mit menschen*, Yiddish for oceans of people. That phrase was widely quoted when recounting the witticisms of my youth. The next stop was the subway to visit my zeyde's sister Anna in Jamaica Queens. This subway ride was not uneventful. Sitting in a corner of the subway car opposite us sat a young couple making out. They were really going at it hot and heavy. I'm glued to the scene. Suddenly, up jumps Zeyde, walks over to the lovers, and says, "Stop it, can't you see there's a young boy over there?" In shock at the command of this stranger, the couple unclinched, just as, in my eyes, things were really getting interesting. In retrospect, this could have been a Bernhard Goetz moment. Zeyde just couldn't shake his disciplinarian experience. He once served as a guard in a New Jersey prison.

Anna's son was an aeronautical engineer. Wow, he designs fighter planes for the air force. What an important and fascinating job. That's what I wanted to be. I later found out that he owned a plumbing supply business. Anyway, for a time, I began to buy and construct model airplanes. "Began" is the operative word here. I started those models, Stinsons, Cessnas, Pipers, etc. and never finished one of them. Too tedious, too delicate a task, and too long to finish. But I seemed to enjoy the process before abandoning that hobby. I didn't know it at the time, but of course, I was happy. I was sniffing all that model airplane glue all day.

One Hanukkah, the family was gathered at my house to celebrate the holiday. After a sumptuous meal, Zeyde left the apartment. We all wondered where he was going. Shortly, he came back with a huge box and announced a gift for cousin Florence. The box contained a beautiful big doll and a dollhouse to match. Everyone applauded and congratulated Florence who was berserk with joy. As the incident was later described, Alvin was standing against the wall, watching all this and tears welling up. Zeyde leaves the room again and goes out to the hall. By now, Alvin bypassed for a Hanukkah gift and left totally out of the celebration, began crying uncontrollably. Zeyde seemed to be gone for an interminable time. Party over and Alvin gets zilch. Apparently, all the other guests were in on the joke. Suddenly, the door opens and in walks Zeyde carrying a huge carton. He sets it down in front of me. All the others start to giggle as I, still sobbing, begin struggling to open the big box. Out comes this gorgeous junior-size pool table with cue sticks and colored numbered balls and all the other accessories, exactly like the big table in Zeyde's club. I start laughing and can't stop. Then my zeyde comes over and gives me a huge hug and a big kiss. My zeyde came through for me, but in his own fashion. After all, they called him Mondle the big teaser. A major player of practical jokes. To this day, my wife thinks that he played a dirty trick on his favorite *einekle* (grandchild), and she holds it against him. Not me. I loved my zeyde and always will.

PART 5

Boot Camp for the Imagination

THE YEAR IS 1935. No TV, no PC, no cell, no video games, no YouTube, no MyFace. I am eight years old. What a wonderful time to be alive. So many books to read. And loads of time to read them. Whenever I am asked where my imagination came from, the answer is basically the same. Every time I cracked open a book or turned on my radio, I was giving my imagination a workout and building a base for the career path I eventually took. What a blessing to be born in a world with no distractions to keep a young mind from developing imaginatively and creatively.

It was not that I was visually deprived. The stories in those books and the dramas enacted on radio were received in high definition on the flat screen of my mind. And all the while, my imagination was growing. I saw movies without going to the movies, and in 1935, watching a movie was not as simple as turning on the TV or slipping a DVD into a player. I saw movies on Lux Radio Theater. For example, *Sorry, Wrong Number*, starring Agnes Moorehead, was memorably created in one hour just using voice and sound effects. I listened and was riveted. Subsequently, I watched the film version with Barbara Stanwyck, and I didn't enjoy it as much. No film could capture the suspenseful narrative of that story better than my own mind.

Much of today's television had antecedents in the early days of radio. *American Idol?* In 1935, anyone who owned a radio listened to *Major Bowes' Amateur Hour. Jeopardy?* In 1935, there was *Dr. I. Q.* A page with a mike roamed the studio audience for contestants, thus came the phrase "I have a lady in the balcony, Doctor." Correct answers were worth between $25 and $100, plus a box of Mars bars or Milky Ways. Every Saturday morning, one could listen and see Grand Central Station for a fascinating tale plucked from the millions of stories in the city. Those episodes rivaled anything now on TV. Before there was *Cheers*, there was *Duffy's Tavern*, "where the elite meet to eat."

At the age of eight, I never had attended Ebbets Field, the Polo Grounds, or Yankee Stadium. Yet I had a seat to all Dodger, Yankee, and Giant games right behind home plate. My hosts who described every detail of the game were Red Barber for the Dodgers, Mel Allen for the Yankees, and Russ Hodges and Frankie Frisch for the Giants. How I loved listening to those games, I even kept score. Some away games were recreated on ticker tape. I saw and enjoyed all the action and was never troubled by the short delay in reality. Hey, President Reagan got his start as a communicator doing ticker tape recreations on radio. Like housewives and many college students hooked on soaps, I was addicted to adventure serializations on radio. My radio, a Philco Superheterodyne, sat on a table next to my bed; and from five in the afternoon to seven in the evening, I was glued to it.

Before frozen TV dinners, there were warmed-up radio suppers, which I ate while listening. Until this day, I believed "superheterodyne" to be a word coined by an advertising copywriter to convey superior radio reception, like the word "halitosis" made up to mean bad breath. But much to my surprise, there is indeed the word superheterodyne, which means, "a form of radio reception in which part of the amplification prior to demodulation is carried out at an intermediate supersonic frequency produced by beating the frequency of the received carrier waves with that of locally generated oscillations." Well, you knew that, didn't you? Despite the dictionary definition, my little Philco performed big-time.

When you tuned in to the radio, you made a commitment. Listening was not optional. Listening was mandatory. So as you put your imagination through a workout when listening to radio, you were also shoring up your ability to listen. And any executive will tell you that one of the biggest shortcomings in business is the inability to listen.

The following are some of the radio programs I regularly followed: What *Star Wars* was to film, *Buck Rogers* was to early radio. Brought to you by Cocomalt. "Hi-ho Silver . . . away!" so opened the *Lone Ranger*, brought to you by Silvercup Bread, made with a whole cup of real milk.

To the sound of Silver's hooves and the stirring William Tell Overture, the Lone Ranger—Ke-mo sah-bee to his trusted companion Tonto—galloped into my home every Monday, Wednesday, and Friday. Tom Mix rode a horse named Tony and was sponsored by Ralston. It was said the oats in Tony's bucket tasted better. Jack Armstrong, the all-American boy from Hudson High, induced me to try Wheaties. From the inner seal of a jar of Ovaltine and fifty cents for S&H, I got a nifty Little Orphan Annie decoder ring and a code for sending secret messages. I can still hear that creaky door on the opening of *Inner Sanctum*, the program that scared the hell out of my brother and me as we huddled on my bed, afraid to breathe.

Sundays at five was reserved for *The Shadow*, or Lamont Cranston and his live-in companion, Margo Lane. "Who knows what evil lurks in the hearts of men? The Shadow knows, heh heh heh." Sponsor, Blue Coal. I was hardly the target audience, but I will always believe that Blue Coal was superior fuel. *I Love a Mystery* was a suspense series featuring Jack, Doc, and Reggie. *Renfrew of the Royal Mounted* opened with the chilling howl of a wolf in the Canadian Rockies. *Omar the Mystic* offered secret *Mystic* handcuffs, which I sent for. No sooner did I unwrap the package than I tried my new trick by inserting a finger in each end of a bamboo tube. Never was I able to solve how to extricate my fingers from the frigging thing, and they had to be cut out of bondage by the school nurse.

At that young age, I was very interested in sponsors and their advertising on the programs I loved, an addiction that stayed with me and eventually helped shape my career. I also enjoyed comedy and variety shows on radio. I listened to Eddie Cantor, Bob Hope, Jimmy Durante, and Fibber McGee and Molly. But the best of them in my estimation was Jack Benny and his ensemble featuring his wife Mary Livingston, announcer Don Wilson, singer and foil Dennis Day, valet and straight man Rochester, and periodically Artie Auerbach, who played Mr. Kitzel and could be counted on to say in a strong Yiddish accent, "Pickle in the middle with mustard on top." Much of Jack's comedy was built around his penuriousness. I heard that original and historic airing, which became arguably the most famous thirty seconds of silence on radio. Jack was accosted by a mugger who demanded, "Your money or your life." After what seemed an eternity, Jack responded, "I'm thinking. I'm thinking." Fast-forward to forty years and I'm writing Jell-O commercials that Jack performed on TV. Could a starstruck kid have a better dream come true?

Henry Morgan aired on radio one night and the next morning became the talk around the watercooler. Morgan, a fresh voice for radio, was kind of a Steve Martin—type comedian, more satire than big yuks. One night he spoofed the popular John Jay Anthony (advice giver à la Dr. Laura) by asking a distraught female caller, "Madam, when did you first realize your husband had left you?" The reply: "We were using less butter in the morning." That bit epitomized Morgan's style of humor. I've borrowed from it ever since.

By stoking my imagination and simultaneously developing appreciation of the creative process, little did I know that I was charting a course for the future. With the demise of radio drama, you would think there would be no way to replicate the experience of my early years. Not exactly the case. Slip an audiocassette into a tape player and listen to a great book on tape and get the best of reading and radio—the twenty-first-century version of boot camp for the imagination.

PART 6

World War and Other Conflicts

WHILE HITLER WAS blitzing his way through Europe virtually unimpeded, I was muddling through high school. Odd to admit, but I was excited about war in Europe. Not to worry, I was a freshman in high school, only twelve, and it'll be over before it ever reaches across the Atlantic. I soon became a passionate student of war, and on a large map spread across my bedroom floor and with the help of newspaper and radio accounts, I was able to follow the conflict and make a game of pushing colored pins from country to country. "Ma, look out you're stepping on Poland"—a move, which might not have been accidental. Both my mother and father experienced Polish anti-Semitism as young adults. My mother fled safely to America with her mother and sister. My father was drafted into the Polish army. One day, he went AWOL, hid in a dense wooded area, and wound up at a farm owned by friendly Poles until he managed to make his way to a freighter bound for America. In Poland, an army deserter was known as a hero. "Wait till Hitler reaches the vaunted Maginot Line in France. That'll be the end of the Wermacht," I told my friends. "Oops. Hitler's army marched through the 'Imagine No Line' like a messer through Brie." There went France. This was not going to be an easy war.

My high school was Eastside High in Paterson. We were the undertakers named for the grounds on which the school was built. No one ever figured out a mascot for this football team. Eastside was the school that gave the world Larry Doby, the first black player in the American League and a Hall of Famer. The school was also to produce the highest-ranking creative officer in the advertising agency business. I was not the most popular man on campus, but I did earn a spot on the student council. Other than that, especially in my freshman and sophomore years, I could have probably been elected class nebbish. Best description of a nebbish: when a nebbish enters a room, everyone says, "Who just left?"

My most notorious accomplishment those early years happened in French class where I insisted on mixing up French and Yiddish, i.e., "Qu'est vus tist do?" or "Hey, what's going on?" Or "Vous a tit dere vay a vous," which translates into "Where does it hurt?" I never did get recognition for inventing a new language, Friddish. I taught Ms. Crooks more Yiddish than she taught me French. I did passably well in other courses, excelling in the ones that I liked and merely passing the classes that bored me.

My personal Abu Ghraib was gym, a mandatory class, which made me nervous. The instrument of torture to which I would confess anything was the rope I had to climb until touching the ceiling of the gym. I thought to myself as I grabbed that thick hunk of a rope with very sweaty palms, *This is not for me. Jews take the elevator.*

Tired of being ignored, I turned to a tactic developed during my early reading and radio days, a sense of humor. If I liked it, and it made me laugh, I adopted humor and tried out my material wherever appropriate. I soon found that a sense of humor characterized my personality and set me apart from my contemporaries. The classroom was the perfect setting for making witty remarks. This became my way of getting noticed and remembered, and it came to be expected of me. But while my classmates would laugh, my teachers wouldn't. The class clown does not get rewarded for untimely interruptions, so my grades began to get very unfunny. Humor also became my trademark during my years as an advertising copywriter. Much to my pleasure, not only was I making kids laugh, I was attracting a new circle of friends, including girls who ordinarily would not acknowledge my existence. It came as a historic revelation, girls like guys who make them laugh. But with all my new notoriety and a welcome bump in female friendships, I managed to go through high school, including the prom, practicing my own particular brand of involuntary abstinence.

With hormones stirring and desire alive, fumbling ineptitude kicked in, and I graduated with my streak unbroken. To make matters worse, in my senior year, acne reared its ugly face. As Buddy Hackett recalled his youth, "God came down, took one look and said, 'You don't have enough tsuris, here take this,' and he threw a big package of pimples at my face." Hackett continued, "So when I was busing in the Catskills one summer, a counselor took me aside and whispered, 'Kid, you want to get rid of those pimples, you need to get shtupped.' When I got back to Brooklyn, I went to a drugstore and asked the pharmacist, 'Hey, mister, can I get shtupped here?' The pharmacist smiled. 'You want shtupped? Not here, kid, not even with a prescription.'"

It was not until several years later, in the backseat of a limo in the parking lot at Frank Scalzo's wedding reception that involuntary abstinence gave way to voluntary decadence. In the interest of full disclosure, my pimples did not go away.

PART 7

Civvies to Skivvies

AFTER DECEMBER 7, 1941, there was no question about America's involvement in a war. We were in it. It was now the Allies—America and Great Britain—versus the Axis—Japan, Germany, Italy. I first heard about Pearl Harbor from a dumbfounded, ice cream—licking patron of Kay's who came flying out of the store with the news. "We've been attacked. We're going to war." First a shock wave then an air of anxiety settled over the neighborhood. What now? Will I have to serve? I was only fourteen at the time. The entire country rallied around President Roosevelt with patriotic fervor not seen again till the nightmare that was 9/11. Nearly everyone wanted to know, "What can I do to help?" There was no shortage of responses: Join the army, the navy, the marines. Buy war bonds and war stamps. Help conserve our resources. Gasoline was rationed as were tires and all things automotive. Women (Rosie the Riveter) were encouraged to work in wartime industries vacated by draftees and enlistees. Don't hoard. As soon as my mother heard that the ingredients of her renowned baked goods would be rationed, she cornered the market on such staples as butter, eggs, sugar, flour, etc. Life without Mary Hampel's honey cake and sponge cake was too horrible to contemplate. Many of Mary's specialties were donated to bond sale events. Support our troops. Write to a serviceman. Celebrities donated their talents to war bond events. The Jimmy Dorsey orchestra featuring Bob Eberly and the gorgeous Helen O'Connell appeared at Eastside High School. Helen O'Connell sang the Dorsey hit "Green Eyes," "Those cool and limpid green eyes." She was looking right at me as she sang. During the war, many items were rationed, and black marketers profited. In our neighborhood, a manufacturer of nylon for parachutes diverted the nylon for hosiery, which women were willing to pay huge amounts for. He was caught and went to jail. The war literally hit home when Herbert Gurantz, son of the corner tailor shop owner, was killed in the invasion of Italy. Back at Eastside High, I was chosen to write a commercial featuring the benefits of buying war bonds and savings stamps. The thirty-second spot talked about helping to win the war now and providing a great investment for the future. I also got to deliver the spot on station WPAT in Paterson. That commercial was the first of hundreds I would later write in my career as an advertising copywriter. My *mishpucha* swelled the station's ratings that morning when I was sandwiched between big band hits. My proud mother alerted the city to listen to Alvin on the radio. Lots of kvelling all around. Pulling a big red radio flyer wagon, a friend and I went house to house collecting pots and pans of aluminum, which was in short supply and desperately needed in the manufacture of aircraft. The women generously donated some of their finest cookware. My mother even parted with the cherished pot in which she made her famous matzo ball soup. If the *New York Post* ran the story: MATZO BALLS AIM AT ENEMY WARPLANES, HOUSEWIVES TAKE POTSHOTS AT NAZI AIRCRAFT, ALUMINUM COOKWARE AIDS WARPLANE PRODUCTION. A while later, some of the women suffered donor's remorse. They felt some of the joy and creativity of meal preparation had left with their pots and pans. So they invented a substitute for cooking. It was called takeout, and it thrives today, nearly seventy years later.

Fast-forward to 1974. As creative director of Benton & Bowles ad agency, I was in Munich to oversee the production of a Texaco commercial to be shown on the telecast of the Olympics. We needed to recruit a band that would dress as Texaco dealers and parade through the streets of Munich playing the Texaco theme song. We auditioned many bands; the best by far was the German Luftwaffe band. So it was that a Jewish kid from Paterson, New Jersey, came to give orders to officers of the German Luftwaffe. "You *vill* follow my instructions." The same Luftwaffe we brought down with the help of aluminum pots and pans donated by the ladies of Eighth Avenue during World War II. Tell that to my fellow junior air raid wardens back in the neighborhood who were wondering, "Whatever happened to Alvin Hampel?" Unfortunately, the Olympics in Munich that year ended tragically with the killing of Israeli hostages.

Kasen's Pants Store billed itself as the world's largest store devoted exclusively to pants. "We can match virtually any fabric." Store windows featured rows of pants lined up like Rockettes in stripes, plaids, solids, herringbones, checks, etc. The windows attracted owners of orphaned suit jackets that needed matching pants to make a suit whole again. Men would stand and lift their legs in worn-out pants to get close to the exhibits in the window. We called them trouser browsers, and when they ventured inside the store, I was one of the salespersons they would encounter. I worked in Kasen's part-time during high school and full time after graduation while deciding what to do about the impending wartime draft. College was totally unaffordable, and frankly, I was tired of school. Many of the matching pants I sold were close if not perfect. "No one will ever notice, especially if you wear the suit at night. Anyway have you ever considered using the jacket as a sport coat, so how about a pair of lovely contrasting slacks?" If you owned two pants suit and burned a hole in the jacket, well, you were SOL. "Wait a minute, how about a beautiful pair of covert cloth slacks to go with that good-looking sweater?" It was at Kasen's that I learned the art of selling. I enjoyed making the sale, helping a poor soul to rescue a suit from the ashbin of worn-out uselessness. Combining selling with writing, my other love, a career of writing advertising copy began to take form.

Every night after work, I would walk around the corner to the back of city hall to wait for the bus home. One night, as I was in line, it started to pour. I was getting drenched when suddenly an umbrella appeared over my head. I turned to see a lovely young girl smiling as she shared her umbrella with me. We boarded the bus and began to chat. This was not an obvious pickup attempt on either part but a friendly exchange between two passengers, one of whom just wanted to help a fellow commuter in distress. For many nights thereafter, my new friend and I sat together and talked and laughed. She talked of her day as a clerk in a lingerie section at Quackenbush's department store in Paterson. Mostly, I would make jokes of her experiences, which naturally afforded many opportunities to be funny. She was petite, not too short and always dressed somberly. She had a sweet, childlike voice, and she giggled and laughed at all my lines, which only encouraged me. The ride would take no more than thirty minutes before my stop. She stayed on to the town of Ridgewood. Then, after about five or six months, our "buscapades" ended as I was off to serve in the navy. Many years later, this innocent but all-too-brief friendship would take a surprising twist that blew me away.

Forty years later, while I was working for Hearst as creative director of *Good Housekeeping*, I received a letter postmarked from a town in Vermont I never heard of. It was from my friend on the bus. I was stunned. How did she ever track me down? She hoped that my life had been happy and successful, but primarily, she wanted to express her gratitude these many years later for helping her when she was going through troubled times. On those trips, she was headed toward a home where she suffered from terrible abuse. I never found out nor cared to ask the specifics. Those bus trips, she wrote, provided much-needed relief from her personal problem, and she credited me for helping her briefly forget the situation that awaited her at the end of the line. I never suspected anything at the time, and while I too enjoyed sitting and chatting with her on the bus, the relationship never blossomed into anything more. We simply parted as good pals with no assurances of a future rendezvous. I responded to her letter and brought her up-to-date on my life since. What followed was even more surprising than her first letter. Turns out she recounted our story to the rabbi in the local synagogue and expressed a desire to convert to Judaism. She took extensive lessons in the religion, even ending up making a *mikvah* (the ritual purification bath), which ultimately sanctions the conversion. My religion never came up in any of our discussions, but I didn't show up on the High Holidays and explained why. At the time of the correspondence, she had five children and planned to raise them Jewish. One time, she sent me a copy of Herman Wouk's wonderful take on Judaism, *This Is My God*. This memorable part of my life doesn't end there. My sweet, charming young lady from the bus had trees planted in my name in Israel. I never heard from her again, but I can only pray that her life as a Jew is filled with happiness and joy.

PART 8

A Sailor's Life for Me

IT WAS THE middle of June 1945; I raised my right hand, swore allegiance to the United States, and the next day, I was on a rickety and musty Lehigh Valley train, which would deliver me to my own gulag for the next three months, Sampson Naval Training Station on beautiful Seneca Lake in the Finger Lake section of upstate New York. I was assigned to F Unit, *F* for Farragut. Luckily, they said, "You didn't get G unit, *G* for Gestapo, the unit led by a sadist who was famous for innovative torture methods and was renowned throughout the navy. How much worse can any unit in boot camp be? First night in the barracks, more than a few new apprentice seamen sat on their bunks and cried. I too thought, *What the frig am I doing here?* But I reminded myself that I was now in the navy, the navy of John Kennedy, George H. W. Bush, John McCain, and Ted Williams. Will I eventually serve on a carrier or a battleship or perhaps a submarine? Maybe a torpedo specialist or a signal man on a carrier. Maybe a gunner on a destroyer. So why do I have to march miles and miles in clunky boots that hugged and chafed my tender flat feet and ankles, areas that never felt anything harsher than white cotton socks and expensive plain toe oxfords. The resulting blisters raised blisters, and only Band-Aids Express Mailed from home kept me from going AWOL. The grinder, the track for running and calisthenics. Jumping jacks and push-ups. And if your ass stuck up, there would be a boot from the squad leader to flatten it. One misstep, like cutting into chow line, and you go on submarine watch, standing at attention facing Seneca Lake, looking for enemy submarines. Bunk not made uptight enough to bounce a coin off, and you are rewarded by swabbing the barracks floor with a toothbrush.

If I'm going to serve on a submarine, why must I navigate the obstacle course, a grisly slog through the woods purposely watered and muddied to get you filthier (we had to launder our own gear) and the obstacles more treacherous and more difficult to negotiate? Me, scale an eight-foot wall? I have trouble getting into an upper bunk. Incidentally, be sure to be wearing undershorts when hopping off an upper bunk or risk "sampsonitis." Those afflicted with sampsonitis left part of their testicles on the uncovered bunk springs. And frankly, the only way for me to cope with that wall was simply to go around it, but not get caught. However, I fooled them down by the creek where officers from the base gathered on one bank to watch skinheads fail to make it swinging on a rope to the other side. This little diversion for the entertainment of the officers produced lots of laughs and catcalls when the poor schnooks dropped into the drink and walked off covered in slime. Not this skinhead. Apprentice Seaman Hampel caught a strongly rebounding rope and like Tarzan, whoop and all, made it with a picture swing to the other side. Hooray, so I'm not such a klutz after all. Like a prisoner knowing the date of parole, I made the best of boot camp, taking R&R whenever I could sneak it in, even learning to laugh at the crap that went on and bonding with some of the guys who shared my interests and foibles. One more big test to pass, and I graduate boot camp as a seaman first class and my permanent assignment in the navy.

I'm in the navy, so there has to be some challenge related to maritime life. Sure enough. In a briefing before being escorted to an enormous swimming pool, we were told to imagine we were on the deck of a burning ship. So each sailor must now climb a ladder fifteen feet to a small platform from which we must jump into the pool, wearing the summer white uniform, the one with all the buttons that you can barely open before peeing in your pants. When you are in the water, you must take off your pants, spread the waist, all underwater, and swing your pants swiftly over your head to fill them with air thus creating a flotation device, which could save your life. Uh-oh, I'm going down with this ship. I can hardly swim, and I'm supposed to execute that lovely intricate maneuver while underwater. If you don't jump, you don't go home on leave, finished with boot camp. So scared shitless, I tucked my hands in my underarms and jumped. Screw it. If I drown, it's their fault. I'm flailing around desperately struggling to get to the surface when something hits me hard in the chest. It's a long pole controlled by a lifeguard standing watch poolside.>

I grab on for dear life and am lifted to the surface, pants still on. Saved, alive, and the navy had *rachmones* (pity) on me because I passed the abandon-ship drill even though bypassing the flotation gimmick.

Best of all, I survived boot camp, and I'm now a seaman first class waiting for my next assignment to help defend the United States from foreign enemies. In my exit interview, I correctly identified warplane silhouettes quickly flashed on a screen. Some I remember: P-51 Mustang, P-47 Thunderbolt, P-38 Lightning, P-39 Airacobra, B-17 Flying Fortress, B-25 Mitchell, B-24 Liberator. I confidently expected to become part of aviation in the navy. I was in for a big surprise.

PART 9

How I Helped Win the War

THE ANSWER: "I was working in a men's clothing store." The question: "What were you doing immediately prior to enlisting in the navy?" I knew right then where my navy career would take me. I would be a storekeeper serving up blue denim fatigues to new recruits. So much for a glamorous life in the US Navy. I might as well be working at old navy. But the good old boy lieutenant who interviewed me put a little twist on my rank. I was shipped off to Storekeeper Disbursing school at Great Lakes Naval Training Station outside of Chicago. It was there that I learned to type and run a Monroe calculator to figure how much each sailor earned for his or her time in service. This was a job for an accountant, not an aspiring advertising writer. I got to know Chicago, a city I loved and later relocated to for a job in advertising. As disappointed as I was with my assignment, my family was pleased. As my mother said upon learning of my move, "What are you complaining about? There's a war going on, and *me ken ge harget vern*. You could get killed out there. You have a nice, safe job. Stay in school, and get good marks."

After Storekeeper Disbursing school, I moved to Saint Louis Naval Air Station at Lambert Field, the major hub for Saint Louis. The war in the Pacific was now winding down, so sailors from the Missouri area were being discharged in greater numbers from the separation center at Lambert. In a small office on base, two fellow SKDs and I calculated separation pay for the happy, new World War II veterans. By any account, I was enjoying good duty. It was said that navy storekeepers freed up WAVES for active duty. Some referred to yeomen and storekeepers as titless WAVES. Nevertheless, I earned a raise in rank to petty officer third class, which entitled me to wear one chevron with crossed keys and a *D* underneath. Since Saint Louis was an army town surrounded by army installations, sailors were welcome newcomers. We were treated as heroes, given special parties, and invited to family dinners. It was in Saint Louis that I discovered the joys of drinking beer with the guys. After a while, beer even began to taste good. So what if you had a little headache the next day? Besides, how could any sailor not like sidling up to the bar and asking for a Griesedieck? That original Saint Louis brew was eventually swallowed up by Falstaff and in a last gasp by Pabst. Even when playing it straight, you were making a joke. I volunteered a theme line, "Griesedieck, smile when you say that, mister." Political correctness was unknown.

Lots of the ladies of Saint Louis favored sailors. One night at a dance, I became a little too amorous on the floor with a leggy, twiggy-looking blonde who didn't so much dance as cling. She clung closer than a dust bunny to a swiffer. I wasn't exactly cling-free either. Finally she whispered those magic words, "Not here." "Not here?" That must mean somewhere else. For once, my imagination didn't betray me. Score one for the raunchy sailor on liberty in Saint Loo. And give an assist to Griesedieck. A week later, I found myself on a train to San Diego to catch a destroyer bound for Yokosuka, Japan. Finally, an adventurous cruise in the Pacific and a duty in a foreign port. I was excited because I hadn't joined up to see America. As fate would have it, the train was late, and my ship sailed without me. I was sent to Camp Elliot in San Diego to await my next assignment. The telegram read, "Report immediately to Long Beach for shipboard duty on the USS *Hector AR7* as Storekeeper Disbursing in the pay office." The ship was named after Hector of Troy in Greek mythology, a legendary figure who was the bravest of all Trojans. At last, a ship I could call mine, but alas, it was docked in San Pedro awaiting reassignment to attend ships wounded in the waning days of the Pacific war. Years later, the *Hector* served in the Korean and Vietnam wars. *AR7* was a fabled repair ship, which earned many honors during its long service. Below decks, the *Hector* housed repair shops of every description. The *Hector* could fix any metallic mess suffered in war. It was most notably known for nursing the battleship USS *Houston* back to life after it was almost sunk by two Japanese torpedo attacks. After the war, the *Hector* became the setting for a popular TV show, *Convoy*. Besides disbursing separation pay to *Hector* personnel being discharged, I was assigned a battle station in case of enemy attack. I learned to pass ammunition to an antiaircraft gun, but happily, it never needed firing. And that's the story of how I just missed winning the Congressional Medal of Honor.

PART 10

The Ascent Begins

ARMED WITH A degree in marketing from NYU, courtesy of the GI Bill, I ventured out into the world to make a career in advertising as a copywriter. In college, I loaded up on advertising courses, which served to introduce me to a world I felt I could succeed in. Ironically, I eked out a C in advertising copy, a course taught by an English professor who knew less about copywriting than a shoemaker. We had barely thirty minutes to write an ad just prior to the bell. The assignments came right out of the textbook and were ridiculous. Yet I persevered in thinking that copywriting was for me. Can you get into advertising just by taking advertising in college? No. Ads themselves are far better textbooks than the ones you get in school. Study print ads, even collect the ones you like. Notice how good provocative headlines get you into the ad and almost force you to read the body copy or the gist of the story. Grabber headlines are to advertising what punch lines are to a joke. Incidentally, humor is one of the most valuable tools for copywriters. Smiles sell. At the time I graduated, the word around school was that jobs in advertising were practically impossible to get, especially for newcomers without any experience. One afternoon, as I was scanning the classifieds in the *Paterson Evening News*, I spotted this: COPYWRITER WANTED. Wow, made for me. As they would say in my family, "It was *bashert*." It was predestined. And that's how I got my first job in advertising at Gordon-Pilling, a small agency in Paterson. It wasn't Madison Avenue; it was Broadway in downtown Paterson on the second floor of the Lindbergh Hotel building, a hot pillow hotel right in the middle of town. There were no candies on the pillow at this high-turnover hooker haven. At Gordon-Pilling, I learned to create mostly newspaper ads for local retailers. "Try This for Sighs" was one headline my bosses thought was brilliant. I knocked out hundreds of newspaper ads and tried to be as original as possible. Standard when I arrived was to filch a copy from services that provided pickup text for every type of product. So eager to get a job as a genuine copywriter, I accepted $40 a week to start. I would have gone to work for nothing just to get the experience. When I asked for a raise, Ed Pilling turned me down. "Al, you're never going to make it as a copywriter." "Screw you, Pilling. I'm out of here." He later fell off a boat in a drunken stupor and drowned. His partner, Cy Gordon, reversed his turndown, and I got the raise. I stayed a few more months. But what if Pilling was right? What if I didn't have it to make it as a copywriter? I never suffered from a shortage of insecurity. It prevailed throughout my life.

While it wasn't Young & Rubicam on Madison Avenue, at Gordon Pilling, I was learning to write copy to deadlines, and I was elated to see my words in print in local newspapers and in various trade magazines. I never got over that thrill. But Pilling's vicious remark sparked a major bout of doubt. Still I persevered. I continued to write. After all, I had been published. My column, "For A Students Only," appeared regularly in the *Criterion* at Eastside and the *Beacon* at Paterson State. It was a humorous look at school life. The column was picked up by schools around the country. I positioned myself as a writer who loved selling. The combination made me an ideal candidate for the career I sought.

In the meantime, I was not just hanging around waiting for something good to come my way. I launched an intensive study of all the advertising around me in all media, magazine, newspaper, radio, outdoor, and direct mail. Often, I thought, *I can do better than this stuff*. I began to read every book in the library on the subject of writing, especially advertising writing. There weren't many. I devoured David Ogilvy's *Ogilvy on Advertising* and Rosser Reeves's *Reality in Advertising*. I practically memorized *A Technique for Producing Ideas* by James Webb Young. I still recommend these books to students of the subject. I was particularly engrossed in the area of creativity, a word which was to become my mantra. As I said, reading books will not transform you into a copywriter, but they will introduce you to the craft and give you some idea of how the masters practiced their skills and wrote beautiful, persuasive advertising copy, copy which helped sell products and move the nation's economy. The work of one ad agency impressed me the most. Doyle Dane Bernbach practically revolutionized the business with its cheeky, clever campaigns for clients, "You Don't Have to Be Jewish to Love Levy's Bread," illustrated by a Native American; "The Ocean Just Became One Third Smaller," illustrated with a torn photo of the Atlantic to show the faster transoceanic route of EL AL Airlines, "No Goose, No Gander" for EL AL's nonstop flight from Europe. The classic Avis campaign, "We're Number Two, We Try Harder," a theme still in use. And the clever Chivas Regal campaign, which won many awards. Of course, the memorable Volkswagen campaign, "Think Small." This was advertising worth emulating. It helped make DDB the hottest agency of the times. Its leader, Bill Bernbach, became my idol. I learned early on that the idea was the bedrock on which all great advertising was rooted. All DDB advertising was based on solid consumer-related ideas. Even without the burdensome research that was to follow, the creative talent was able to tap into basic consumer wants, always interpreted with wit or humor.

An aside: As I write this in February of 1908, I must cite a line currently running for Cadillac, "When you turn your car on, does it return the favor?" A brilliant piece of copy and an example for aspiring writers to study. Incidentally, there is no big secret to developing writing skills. You learn writing by writing. This bit of advice led me to only those jobs where I could keep on writing.

PART 11

Tuxedo Junction

A COUPLE OF FLOORS up from Gordon-Pilling in the Lindbergh Hotel building, one could rent formal wear for men at Damoff's, a store run by Harry Gross. In my spare time from copywriting downstairs, I hung out upstairs with Harry. The place was completely surrounded by large pipe racks that housed the various styles and sizes of tuxedos for rent. Not only the suits, but all the accessories that completed a formal outfit. As I wrote in a promotional letter I produced for Harry, "Everything from Your T Zone to your Toe Zone." Weddings, proms, New Years, banquets, balls, inaugurations were busy times for Damoff's. When not busy, Harry and I had lots of time to bond. We had long and spirited conversations mostly larded with lots of laughs. We both had the rare ability to laugh at ourselves. Harry Gross became a best friend. Funny how shared hypochondria cements friendships. There wasn't a deadly symptom that he didn't have and that I didn't catch. But we laughed our way through our diseases even as we sorted through the returned tuxes, many with every stain and every vileness remains of a night the wearer couldn't even remember.

President Clinton was impeached on the evidence on a blue dress. The Passaic County DA could have indicted every renter of Damoff's tuxedos. What stories those garments could tell. There's an idea, "Tuxedo Tales." So in the summertime, it was only natural that my good friend and I headed for vacation together. Where else, but the Catskills, the Jewish Alps. Some men go to mountains to hike or fish or hunt or to camp or engage in other outdoor activities. Harry and I went to the mountains to meet girls because that's where the girls went to meet guys. The mutual motivation made for terrific days, and if you got lucky, memorable nights. The Catskills were the Club Med of the times. You had outdoor activities galore and nightly entertainment often consisting of new young comedians honing their skills for bigger things to come. It was not unusual for appearances by Milton Berle, Buddy Hackett, Woody Allen, Jan Murray, Red Buttons, Mel Brooks, and Alan King.

After the show, music and dancing every night. There were dozens of hotels flourishing in those days, none more famed than the big two, Grossinger's and Concord. Harry and I were attracted to less fancy, but still considered five-star hotels like Brickman's, Kutsher's, Laurel-In-The-Pines, and any resort that claimed to be that year's most swinging spot. In addition to all the activities that the hotel tummler, the social director, could grab you for, always including the daily competition of Simon Says, there was the *food*.

Way before cruise ships claimed choke-a-horse cuisine, you could easily tack on five pounds with all-you-can eat dining on the finest Jewish specialties. Your two-week vacation in the Catskills was like cruising on the good ship *Ess, Ess, My Kind* (as in "sinned"). Eat, eat, my child. The favorite after-dinner drink was Brioschi. The table you were assigned to in the dining room was critical. Check out the girls. Not so hot, switch. Play musical tables.

The first night of dining, everyone was dressed to make a great impression. It was time for checking things out. My good buddy Harry points to me, convulsed with laughter. There I sit trying my best to look like Cary Grant in my brand-new light blue houndstooth sport coat, elbows suavely draped over the table with all the tickets usually sewn on to a new garment clearly displayed for all to see: Size 38, all wool, UnionMade. Soon, the whole table was in stitches. So much for first impressions. My dad bought the sport coat for me at the employee discount store of the Botany Mills in Passaic where he then worked. Whenever I wore that jacket, the ladies of the table would look for the labels. It was determined that I was a nice guy who wore his size on his sleeve. About food in the Catskills, I am reminded of a joke told by Freddy Roman. A little old woman, a guest of the hotel, was complaining to the manager. "The food is not so good this year. Used to be better. And the portions are so small."

PART 12

Swept Off My Feet

After our Catskill vacations, Harry and I realized that being nondancers put us at a disadvantage in the competitive quest for female partners in the mountains. Harry danced with the rhythm of rigor just a little before mortis set in. Hampel resembled an old man frantically searching for the nearest urinal so as not to miss an important part of the movie. Thus, it was not surprising to find both of us taking dancing lessons from the Betty Robbins School of Dance in Pompton Lakes. Harry enrolled with his wife Roma and several other couples. Yes, Harry was married. I was the single man dragged into the venture with mixed feelings.

Being the spare, I was paired with Ms. Betty as she demonstrated the intricate steps of the rumba, mambo, cha-cha, some tango, and even a review of the old standby fox-trot. After three or four sessions, much to my amazement, I found myself beginning to enjoy the art of dance. And why not? I got to dance with the teacher one night a week. Betty was an attractive brunette who regularly drew second glances, and she displayed the lissome moves of a professional dancer, which indeed she was. Betty Robbins was a former Roxyette, the Roxy theater's chorus line answer to Radio City's Rockettes. She had a cleft in her chin, and the rest of her pretty face could never be mistaken for other than Irish. What was it about me and Irish girls? Abie's Irish Rose? She was in her midthirties with a ten-year-old daughter. I was twenty-three and very susceptible to being swept off my feet by an older woman.

Recent stories in the news tell of sexy adult teachers forming illicit relationships with underage male students. In my case, I was a willing adult pupil experiencing the time of his life. When the group lessons were finished at about 10:00 PM, I would invariably stay after school at the studio for some private tutoring. As my private lessons grew to two days, three days, and more a week, there was no mistaking where this pupil-teacher match was headed.

As I look back, I was an arm candy for the lovely, more mature Betty Robbins while becoming a hell of a dancer. Yes, we could have qualified for *Dancing with the Stars*. As graceful as we were at executing those intricate steps, we eventually fell, and fell hard. While ours was that rare joyous relationship, in my heart I knew it would never pan out as Betty hoped it would.

Word soon got around that Hampel was going with someone, a *shiksa* (non-Jewish girl) no less. Gossip in the neighborhood had it that the Hampel family was prepared to sit *shiva* (a mourning ritual for the dead). Parting was not such sweet sorrow. It was traumatic and tearful. Betty recovered and went on to remarry while continuing to convert klutzes like me into reasonable dancers. I was left with a much-needed infusion of self-confidence. According to the adage, "When two hearts race, there can be no loser." At the end of our affair, we were winners by just being in the race.

PART 13

Discouraged but Undeterred

IT DIDN'T TAKE an MBA to figure out that I would eventually want to leave Madison Avenue in Paterson for Madison Avenue in New York. As they say in baseball, "Going from the minor leagues to the bigs." I began to scour the classifieds in every newspaper I could get my hands on including the powerhouse classifieds of the *New York Times*. I was determined to keep piling up copywriter experiences no matter where an appropriate job opportunity surfaced. My philosophy could be summed up in five words, "Alight where you can write." I never gave up the habit of expressing thoughts as if they were slogans or theme lines in an advertising campaign.

I looked into any job opportunity that would help fatten my résumé and afford me samples. Copywriting is a business of samples. The interviewer sitting across the desk isn't going to hire you on your looks. Advertising demands to see what you've done in other jobs. Show him or her what you've written, proof that you have some experience writing advertising for publication. Or totally lacking advertising writing, show writing for an English course, for a local or school newspaper, or writing of any kind to show that you can at least string words together intelligently. And if creativity shines through, all the better. I interviewed for a job at Bamberger's, the Newark department store. Certainly, my sample ads written at Gordon & Pilling, although standard retail copy in most instances, would qualify me for a job at a retail giant like Bam's. At least I had some, albeit meager, experience in retail advertising. How could they not snap me up? Or so I thought. I created ads with all the right headlines, "Sale, Save, New, At Last, Now, Back to School, A Gift for Giving, etc."

The top floor of the imposing Bam's building was the location of the advertising department. The offices looked old and run-down, much like the newsroom of a weekly newspaper—people scurrying about carrying tear sheets or layouts for approval. Lots of chatter and the clatter of typewriters. Tear sheets and mats adorned the walls. Finally, I'm ushered into the office of the ad manager. She's behind the most cluttered desk I've ever seen. We exchanged small talk, and she seemed to be a nice person. About ten minutes of chitchat where I presented my credentials, schools, residence, hobbies, writing background, why I wanted to be a copywriter for such a distinguished store, etc. Going along fine, I think, and *zap*, she hits me with the question, "Have you ever heard of a women's fashion designer [I don't remember the name], and what current fashion that's made her famous?" Duh? "How do you expect to write fashion copy?" My only response was, "The ad didn't say anything about fashion copy." I never even got to show her my slender book of ads written at Gordon & Pilling. As I sheepishly backed out of her office, I thought, *This lady reminds me of Mrs. Butterworth in a housedress, and she's asking me about fashion.* On the way home, I think of what I should've said, *Who's the leading designer of men's shoes, and what's his current best-selling design? Or who plays second base for the Boston Red Sox?* I got to thinking about what I call the do-over words, "should've," "would've," "if only."

How different history and our personal stories would be if the do-overs would or could kick in with a second chance to make things right. As I write this, Senator Hillary Clinton would love to do over her misstatement about braving sniper fire in Bosnia. And Senator Barack Obama would love to do over his proclamation of "bitterness" as the reason why many voters turned to guns and religion. For that statement, he was tabbed as an elitist, which helped contribute to his defeat in the Pennsylvania primary.

The Bernice Fitzgibbon wannabe (Fitzgibbon the doyenne of retail newspaper advertising having perfected the craft at Macy's and Gimbels) at Bam's in Newark ignominiously handed me the first rejection in my quest to become an advertising copywriter. Rejections suck, but I was undeterred.

PART 14

Last Stop Before New York

WHIPPANY? SOUNDS LIKE the call of the dominatrix. It's a town on Route 10 in Morris County, New Jersey, headquarters of Suburban Propane Gas Company, largest distributor of liquefied petroleum (bottled) gas in the East. Here in a rather weird detour from the New York I was heading for, I became assistant advertising manager because I needed a job, and the title would look good on my résumé. A twenty-mile commute from home in Paterson, I went to work at a desk in a sea of desks that comprised the main office of Suburban Propane. It would be years before I earned a private office in an ad agency, where I ultimately lusted to create advertising on a national scale. It was 1953. I was twenty-six and writing, which any writer will tell you is what you must keep doing if you want to be a writer. Nothing glamorous, but a chance to be working away from my craft gaining more samples and getting paid for it. The product was bottled gas, so the ads and brochures I wrote promoted the gas and the service Suburban provided as well as the brand name of the gas appliances they sold. Kvetch (complain) as I did about the mundane nature of the work, I was getting a good experience. And I got to edit the company newsletter, *Suburban Propane News*. This was a monthly publication dedicated to enhancing employee morale by communicating the feeling of family. The idea was to incorporate lots of photos with squibs of weddings, birthdays, births, even obits, sports news of company teams, and any little tidbit that would be of interest to fellow employees. Woe is to the editor who omitted a recent snapshot or what was considered news from any employee in any Suburban office. Items were often as earthshaking as "Peggy Galvin of our home office is now cruising around town on four new Goodyears on her Ford. You could hear Peggy coming to work from the hum of her new shoes."

Suburban also distributed a fertilizer called anhydrous ammonia, which was stored and shipped in the same kinds of tanks as LP gas. So I got to write advertising addressed to farmers about a fertilizer that could turn asparagus spears from the dimensions of Bic ballpoints to the size and shape of Montecristo No. 3 cigars. This product was great stuff and resulted in the raising of bumper crops for the farmers who used it as fertilizer. The head of the agriculture division of Suburban liked my work as it helped increase sales of anhydrous ammonia and made him look good. But he didn't like me personally since the time I pointed out one day that his fly was open.

No ad I ever wrote created such an instant tzimmes (a troublesome situation) as the ad headlined, "The Story of a Little House Taken by Storm." It was written in the form of a fable and told of the horrendous inconveniences created during a power outage in an electrical storm. There have always been disagreements over which was the best cooking fuel, gas or electric. Top chefs preferred gas for its controllability and superior searing qualities. The ad in question was illustrated with a bolt of lightning over power lines crudely drawn by our in-house artist. With just one insertion in the local Morris County weekly, the stuff hit the fan. Mark Anton, a state legislator and president of Suburban Gas, received an irate letter from his counterpart at the local electric utility, stating something to the effect, "Dear Mr. Anton, our files contain dozens of photo of lovely homes completely destroyed by propane gas explosions. I'm sure you would not like to see these photos published, so in the interest of fair play, please refrain from running the ad, 'The Story of a Little House Taken by Storm' I'm sure you are not interested in an ongoing battle of your worthy product versus ours." Thus ended the incipient conflict precipitated by an ad I wrote. Though the conflict was over, I was proud of my part in tripping a war of energy sources. It was one of my first triumphs and a graphic example of the power of advertising.

PART 15

A New York Job with a Lifetime Benefit

PASSING THOUGHT: I just saw a window on Lexington Avenue that featured a sign reading, "Flyer Boy Wanted." What an odd medium for air force recruitment. I'd like to say I planned every step of my career. Not. Between jobs, I often had doubts and misgivings. Am I good enough for this kind of work? What if I never get another job in advertising? At one point, I even called my friend Bobby Gray, who was then a teacher, and asked what qualifications I would need to teach. As luck would have it, along came an offer from Amos Parrish and Co. What's an Amos Parrish? It's America's leading consulting firm for retailing and merchandising. Sounded good, and best of all, it was on Fifth Avenue in New York, only one block from Madison Avenue, my ultimate destination.

I interviewed with the head of the department store, consulting one Murray Rae. He reminded me of George Raft and talked like him. After hemming and hawing, he fingers his chin and murmurs, "OK, kiddo, we'll engage you. We're not going to marry you, but we'll watch and see how things work out." More encouraging words were never spoken. So with that vote of confidence, I took the job as a copywriter for the leading department stores at a salary of $6,000 a year. Amos Parrish became an opportunity that would lead to valuable retail experience as well as an encounter that would change my life.

For department stores such as Meier & Frank, Woodward and Lothrop, Burdines, Hecht's, Carson Pirie Scott, Hudson's Bay, Foley's, Marshall Field's, etc., I gave names to promotional events, mostly sales, and wrote the introductory full-page newspaper ads. "Whale of a Sale," "Honey of a Sale" for Bear's, "Humongous Sale," and for Christmas, "B. Altman Has a

Gift for Giving," "At Lord & Taylor Back to School is Cool." Somebody had to write those gems. The projects were known as attacks, and the salespeople sold them with little concern for timing, so you were always working against short deadlines. If the staff had its way, the attacks would be lodged against the guys who promised unrealistic delivery dates. The stores needed enough lead time to get ready for the event and line up the hundreds of sale items, particularly the door busters, those small-type, boldface listings that featured the largest savings of the sale and produced the most traffic.

I worked in a big room with four guys who crunched numbers for the sales goals set during the promotional events. I was the lone creative. We hardly saw Murray Rae, the department head. Instead, he delegated his supervisory responsibility to Dorothy. In essence, she ran the department making sure the work was on schedule. Because she cajoled, pushed, and prodded to get the projects finished in time, Dorothy was not the most beloved person in the company. As she made her rounds to make sure deadlines were met, Dorothy sometimes lost her cool, raised her voice, and became officious and irritating. She was always firm but polite when checking my work. I found her demeanor rather amusing. The other guys she was shepherding didn't. Their resentment led to some charming nicknames, the nicest of which was the Dragon Lady. The rest would have made George Carlin's infamous list of seven. I enjoyed eyeing this chic and attractive young woman play boss to a bunch of wise guys who just naturally resented being told what to do by a girl they wouldn't mind getting to know better.

While Dorothy occasionally pissed me off, she was too lovely looking to ignore. I decided there must be a softer, more endearing side to the Dorothy that I saw in that office, so I took it upon myself to find it. Fifty years later, three great kids, three wonderful grandchildren, and I think I know the real Dorothy. Despite some potholes along the way, it's a voyage I would do all over again. These days, Dorothy Hampel directs her rants at politicians on television.

It's not that my wife doesn't occasionally revert to earlier form, but by now, we just reminisce and laugh. A principle I picked up at Amos Parrish served me well in later years, especially in one important meeting with

Sears, Roebuck execs while I was in Chicago at Foote Cone & Belding. The discussion was about Sears's newspaper advertising and how the agency could help improve its effectiveness. I chimed in, "Something I learned a long time ago when I worked at Amos Parrish and Co., promote most what sells best." One female Sears' senior marketing executive at the table spoke up, "I agree with that, and we should be doing more of it. You worked at Amos Parrish? I used to attend those fashion clinics. They were fabulous." With that meeting, I became a consultant to the Sears account, which was one of Foote Cone & Belding's largest pieces of business and one which was constantly rumored to be in trouble. We did not lose the Sears account while I was executive creative director of the agency.

PART 16

Hangin' with Kong

PASSING THOUGHTS: SIGN in a Second Avenue laundry, "We do shirts better. Cost the same as your favorite grand latte." Advertisers who insist on casting kids to spout complicated financial copy in their TV commercials end up with gibberish and are wasting their money. Cutesy but totally lacking credibility. Might as well use a parrot and save on residuals. Would you buy life insurance from Ian, my eight-year-old grandson? AIG thinks you would. How did P&G ever transition from kindly old Mr. Whipple who with a wink would so politely ask customers to refrain from squeezing Charmin, to animated bears in the woods? At a lunch with the ad people the other day, not one of us could rationalize the current Charmin campaign other than to consider it an outgrowth of the well-known expression, "Does a bear poop in the woods?" This is from Procter & Gamble, the most politically correct of all advertisers? We could only conclude if it's selling toilet paper, don't ask.

At a floor high in the fifties of the Empire State Building in 1956, I went to work for Ralf Shockey and Associates. Shockey was a sales promotion outfit with a handful of creative people, writers, and art directors. Ralph Shockey was a well-known sales promotion specialist who, because of his reputation and connections, attracted blue chips who desperately needed promotional help that they were not getting from their ad agencies. So it was here that I got to create ideas and collateral material that would supplement the advertising produced by ad agencies. The accounts included Chrysler, Corning, GE, various Seventh Avenue fashion houses. I remember writing a booklet for GE to be distributed to retailers entitled, "Thirty One Ways to Promote GE Small Appliances In Store." Believe me, it was a strain to reach thirty-one, and I wonder if any store ever even implemented half the ideas. We even designed sales meetings for our accounts. I was finally working on some big league stuff, a far cry from Winthrop's Vacuum Cleaners and Stenchever's Shoes in Paterson. And the views from my office in the Empire State Building were spectacular.

At Shockey, I learned to do writer's roughs, visualizations of the copy I wrote and how I expected it to complement the planned illustrations and folds of a mailing piece, for example. Size, number of pages, where pictures fit, headlines, and subheadlines. I was not doing the art director's job but was pointing him or her in the direction the finished layout should take. As a copywriter, I thought that my turf was the wording and the layout, and visuals were the exclusive province of the art director. Instead, I began to see the importance of thinking visually even before a word was ever written. Verbalization and visualization in advertising are intertwined, and any good copywriter is skilled in visualizing, and vice versa for a good art director. In my career, I have seen art directors write some of the best lines, and copywriters come up with the most arresting layouts. For example, an art director came up with the line for P&G's Rely tampons, "It Even Absorbs the Worry." An ad I wrote while at Y&R began with a tight close-up of a bowl of Jell-O Chocolate Pudding to depict smoothness, "Jell-O Believes You've Taken Enough Lumps In Your Life."

One day while in the john on our floor in the Empire State, in came Joel Frede who was Shockey's right-hand man. While standing at the urinal next to me, he says, "How you doing, Alvin? You know we just lost one of our biggest accounts. We're going to have to cut back. I'm sorry, Alvin, but I have to ask you to leave." Here I was taking a leak, and suddenly, I'm in shock at Shockey. "Are you kidding? But, Joel, you just hired me about three months ago." "I know, Alvin, but it's LIFO, last in first out." All I could say was, "I can't believe this. The clients are buying my work. Everyone thought I was doing a good job." A little later back in the office, he comes over, nudges me with his elbow, and quietly says, "Hey, Alvin, forget what I told you in there. It's a mistake." Apparently, when word got around the office that I had been fired, the creative people practically assaulted Joel and let him know he blew it. "You fired the wrong guy." So about fifteen minutes after I was fired, I was rehired. And as for the method of dismissal, Joel Frede really pissed me off.

Russ was a public relations specialist at Shockey. One day, he invited me to join him for a drink after work when he was meeting Walter Weiner, head of public relations at Young & Rubicam. "You'll like Walter, and maybe he can help you get a hearing at Y&R." At the time, I felt, "Well, another one of those help-you-get-a-job introductions, but what the hell, I'll go and meet the man."

PART 17

Is This a Joke?

PASSING THOUGHT: AN update on my brother Daniel, the brainy one in the family. Remember he chose a career in electrical engineering while I went on to become a huckster. Dan is now a hotshot consultant with Booz Allen Hamilton. From a recent news release, "Booz Allen Hamilton has been awarded a $149.5 million, multi-year delivery order to provide technology, program management and engineering support to the U.S. Army's Space and Terrestrial Communications Directorate under the Strategic Services Sourcing." Dan Hampel, program manager, said, "This project is the largest modernization effort in Army history and one of the most complex networking of systems across the joint services." Whatever that all means, but it sounds really important. All I can say is we can all be grateful Dan is on our side. Let it be recorded that I contributed to increased recruitment for the US Air Force with the advertising slogan, "Aim High." Dan and I always competed going back to those fiercely contested cribbage games we played in the bedroom we shared on Twenty-Third Street in Paterson. Last time I looked, he was beating me by hundreds of games. But you had to count holes, and he was always strong on math. I was a word man.

Late in the summer of 1957, after a brief vacation in Fire Island, I returned home to find a letter from Young & Rubicam waiting. This can't be, I immediately thought, *Y&R writing to me?* As my trembling fingers tore the envelope, I imagined all kinds of scenarios. Could this be my first rejection notice from the most prestigious New York ad agency even before I was interviewed? But then again, a rejection from Y&R is better than an acceptance from Ted Bates. Go figure. The letter requested that I call for an appointment. Dorothy recalls that I started celebrating as if I got the job. "But just a minute," she reminded me. The letter is signed by a Harry

Rubicam, and isn't he dead? This has to be a joke. Someone is playing a trick on me.

True to his word, Walter Weiner passed my résumé on to the right person at Y&R. Or did he? Sure enough, there was a Harry Rubicam, head of human resources for the creative departments. He turned out to be a nephew of Ray Rubicam, one of Y&R's founders. He was a grandfatherly gent who talked to me about the greatness of Y&R and what a wonderful place it was to work there. Like I needed to be advised. Harry Rubicam introduced me to Bob Work, manager of the copy department. We had about a fifteen-minute chat, and browsing through my résumé, he asked why I had moved around so much. "No, sir, those are not places, they're the accounts I have worked on."

Bob Work was completely bald and much younger than he looked. He was a beloved friend of the creative departments and a senior member of the all-important plans board, the body that had final approval on critical campaigns for the agency's leading clients. Bob Work offered me a job in sales promotion at a starting salary of $8,000 a year. The cliché that I would have paid him to work at Y&R in any capacity could not have been a more accurate expression of my elation as I left the building at 285 Madison Avenue that sunny summer afternoon. Look, Ma, I made it, and I didn't have to work my way up from the mail room, one of advertising's more traditional starting jobs. So what if I started out in sales promotion, a tangential department that helped supplement the more glamorous media of print, radio, and the fledgling medium, TV. I was in the house, and that was what mattered. For days, I walked around my old neighborhood and places where I used to work, looking for friends and anyone who would listen. "Yeah, I got a new job at Young & Rubicam. You've heard of it, right?"

My early impressions: Every day I commuted by bus from Wayne, New Jersey, and later Ridgewood to the Port Authority Bus Terminal and a walk east on Forty-First Street. I couldn't wait to go to work in the place I considered a cathedral of creativity. Not a new agency in a new building, Y&R showed signs of aging, its walls dull green (green for Dartmouth, CEO's Sig Larmon, a renowned alumnus and a golfing buddy of President Eisenhower). Its furniture, utilitarian and a little shopworn from the squirming and fidgeting of the rear ends that were broken coming up with winning campaigns. From those modest surroundings came such memorable campaigns as Bert and Harry Piel, the Remington shaving a peach, Jell-O's Chinese baby (trying to eat Jell-O with chopsticks), Lay's Potato Chips, Kent with the Micronite Filter, The Temptation of Beautyrest, Breck, J&J baby products, Excedrin headache, Borden's Elsie, General Electric, Chrysler, General Cigar, Modess Because, Band-Aids. One new and naive copywriter submitted a headline to her supervisor, "Never Neglect the Smallest Prick." The ad never ran.

PART 18

And Then I Wrote

PASSING THOUGHT: ON a recent episode of *Mad Men*, the Emmy-winning show on TV, the Maytag client was agitated when someone on the show Maytag sponsored referred pejoratively to a character as an agitator. "You can't do that when the exclusive feature of our washing machine is an agitator." Maytag launched a mild protest.

Segue to the 1960s when Y&R put together a TV special for Chrysler, one of the agency's largest clients. As Harry Belafonte came on stage to greet Petula Clark, a beautiful blond pop star from England, he put his arm around her waist. He might just as well have embraced an IED (improvised explosive device), but what exploded was the Chrysler client. "That black man touched that white girl on our show. There go our dealerships in the south." The telephone switchboard lit up. "I'll never buy another Chrysler car." Chrysler threatened to take the account from Y&R and demanded the account executive in charge be fired. This was a live show so editing was not possible. "He never did that in the rehearsal" was all that Colgan Shlank, the poor account guy, could feebly explain. After a while, calmer heads prevailed, and the incident became history. Colgan Shlank kept his job, and thereafter, a policy of "no touching" was strictly enforced. Today, we had a black man who ran for president of the United States. How things have changed. Or have they?

Meanwhile, as the new kid on the block at Y&R, I was enjoying doing the grunt work that senior writers were shielded from since their work on ads for major media paid the bills. Sales promotion and trade advertising didn't. One of my first assignments was to write a four-page newspaper insert announcing the Drackett company's TV sponsorship of an oater called Wagon Train, starring Ward Bond. The Gulf account had a huge appetite for collateral material. So in concert with a talented art director, Kevin McNally, we ground out such Gulf station point-of-purchase materials as opening day announcements, highlighting the appearance of clowns, free balloons, kiddie carnivals, and all the usual hoopla designed to attract motorists to come in and fill up. Someone had to think up that stuff and write the words. Not exactly an award-winning material, but I just kept reminding myself that I was a copywriter at Y&R, and a lot of other copywriters out there were not. They would have gladly traded their jobs at other ad agencies for mine, but not at my salary.

Dermott McCarthy, then copy chief who later became a dear friend and supporter, would never fail to remind everyone that Al Hampel will forever be remembered for writing those immortal words that brought more people into Gulf stations than any other incentive. "Al wrote 'Men' and the copy on the other door, 'Women.'"

How was I ever going to break into the corps of elite writers and thinkers around me? They were hot and experienced but not too snobbish to offer advice to a tyro. I might have been a pain in the butt, but those senior Y&R stars took the time to chat and inform the junior who just dropped into their midst. I devised a plan on how I would get noticed. It was a simple strategy. I considered all the talent around me as competition. I was determined to win by working harder and never being satisfied with the first ideas that came to mind, but to keep going for something better. Later in life, I designed a button in the form of a Stop sign that said "Don't Stop." I assumed the big idea was out there, waiting to be found, and I was determined to keep going till I reached that "aha, that's it" solution to a creative problem. My strategy for advancement was not a new plan in the business world, but it did entail sacrifice. I devoted almost all my spare time to thinking about a better line or word or concept. I thought about my assignment on the bus, while walking to the office, watching TV, before bed, upon waking, even on vacation with my family. Was I being fair to them, or myself for that matter? Vacation was supposed to be a time of diversion and respite from the stresses of the job. My wood shedding[1] problem took a toll on my health and my role as a father of two young boys. Bob Work who hired me, said, "You're not being fair to yourself."

Eric Clapton was a well-respected guitarist in Britain. Yet there was still a desire to get better. He took time off to practice for two years straight.

---

[1] To practice and practice and practice till you get it right.

I adopted the principle of wood shedding as a way of getting better at the craft of copywriting. Working on the General Electric dishwasher account, I named an exclusive new feature, "Power Shower." It was readily accepted by the GE client and was immediately incorporated into all GE dishwashers, where it lives to this day. The GE client was so pleased he gave me a GE radio and stipulated that I work on all GE appliance accounts. If the client likes you, you gain leverage in an ad agency.

The account executives made sure you stuck with their business and spread the word about a creative young kid in sales promotion. The assignment was to create a statement enclosure that was sent to Gulf credit card holders with their monthly bills. Kevin McNally designed the piece. I named it "Between Tankfulls," a masthead at the top of a small newsletter that is still mailed to Gulf credit card holders. With four words, "Power Shower" and "Between Tankfulls," I began the building of my reputation at Y&R. Before long, I found myself working on trade advertising; the ads that appeared in special journals circulated among retailers and distributors of products and services. This category is now known as business-to-business advertising and these days enjoys a more prominent role in the marketing mix.

For *Life Magazine*, I wrote a trade ad featuring a testimonial from Arnold Palmer. To get the story, leading photographer Ormond Gigli and I flew to Pittsburgh and drove to Latrobe to interview Palmer about being a regular reader of *Life*. We had to backtrack to downtown Latrobe to pick up a copy of the magazine. There was none in the Palmer house. I told Palmer I would make sure he would get a complimentary subscription. He called out to his wife, Winnie, "Win, this man is going to get us a prescription [sic] to *Life*." Such was my introduction to the veracity of testimonial advertising. I got the story, Gigli got his pictures, but the trip did not end there.

Palmer, who was then learning to fly, insisted on flying us from Latrobe to the Pittsburgh airport. We crammed into the back of a single-engine Cessna with Palmer at the controls. No sooner did we lift off and the plane nose-dived back to earth. Gigli dug his fingers into my knee and wouldn't let go. All I could think was, my first trade ad would be my last. Only the instructor sitting beside Palmer safely corrected Palmer's error. We still had to sweat out the flight as Palmer again took over in order to log some flight time for his license and flew the rest of the flight to Pittsburgh where the instructor landed the plane. Today, Arnold Palmer flies his own jet to all his tournaments. To think, I helped him get his pilot's license.

PART 19

An Auspicious Beginning

PASSING THOUGHT: EVER since I decided on advertising copywriter as a career, I dreamed of one day working in a Madison Avenue ad agency. Now that I'm officially a copywriter at Y&R, an agency many considered the most creative of the large ad agencies, I regularly pinch myself and ask, "Is this really happening, or am I still dreaming?" Since this memoir is the story of a kid from Paterson who made it in the big leagues of advertising and made it big in the big leagues, I'm about to embark on the "I/me chronicles," a recounting of my work at the job I loved.

So it's not because I have a big ego that I will regale with my hits and even a miss or two, but because this is the work that helped propel me to the top. By the way, I'd rather have a big ego and display it than be known as a *shmendrick* (a meek, ineffectual milquetoast). I left the world of trade advertising in a blaze. Assigned to the Simmons Beautyrest account, I immersed myself in the world of mattresses, and particularly, the merits of Beautyrest. No one could convince me that there was a better mattress in the world. I knew Beautyrest from the innersprings to the ticking, and to learn how the trade approached the selling of Beautyrest, I spent time on the selling floor at Bloomingdale's. From this research, a four-page all copy ad was born with the headline, "How One of the Most Expensive Mattresses Became the Biggest Selling Brand in the World," over my byline, *By Alvin Hampel.* Copywriters normally create anonymously, but early in my copywriting career, I had my one and only byline.

My next assignment for Simmons Beautyrest was to craft a campaign aimed at the salespeople who were asked to sell fair-traded Beautyrest for $39.50 while the competition was selling mattresses for as low as $25 and claiming they were as good. Here is where I went off in a different direction from the straight, factual promotional work I was turning out. I decided to go clever and get bold and edgy. Ever since grade school, I was known to be clever or funny, even a cutup at times, and that description stuck with me through college. Indeed, it was the reason I was first attracted to advertising, a business built on cleverness. I learned later on that cleverness might have been a way to grab attention, but cleverness without selling might have been entertaining but was really a waste of money. The Beautyrest trade campaign featured such sassy headlines as, "Anyone Who sells a $25 mattress deserves the $2 dollar profit," "The backbone is connected to the money belt," "Price isn't the only thing that gets cut," an ad featuring the salesman with his finger crossing his neck as in a suicide gesture. "Invite the customer to test a Beautyrest but be sure to leave a wakeup call." Each ad was illustrated with full executives at Y&R. His grumpy, sell-Beautyrest-or-look-for-work mug fit the campaign perfectly. A few months after the campaign broke, I was called on stage at an awards luncheon sponsored by a retailing group and was awarded first prize for retail trade advertising. Jack Grier accompanied me on stage and got a rousing ovation too.

PART 20

As If It Was Yesterday

PASSING THOUGHT: ONE day, as I was watching the Boston Red Sox on TV, up to bat came a center fielder called Coco Crisp. My five-year-old granddaughter Erin Maeve said, "Coco Crisp, what a funny name." I told her his mother didn't know what to call him when he was born, so happening to gaze at a box of cereal on the kitchen table she thought, *Why not?* And that's how he got his name. With one of her exuberantly beguiling laughs, lovely little Erin quipped, "What if it was Froot Loops?"

It's 2:00 a.m. in Los Angeles, and I'm fast asleep in my hotel room when the phone jars me awake. Operator: "Mr. Al Hampel. I have a call from a Mr. Hoagy Carmichael." Hear that, Scaz, Maish, Harry, Bull, Squirrel, Tommy, Bobby, and all you other guys on Eighth Avenue in Paterson? The great Hoagy is calling Al Hampel. He wants to know if he can change one word of the lyric in a voice-over to introduce Log Cabin Country Kitchen Butter Syrup, a product to compete with Mrs. Butterworth. "Get that, you guys. Hoagy Carmichael is asking Al Hampel if he can change one word of Hampel's lyric. I say, "Let me hear how it sounds, Hoagy." So Hoagy Carmichael sings the new lyric on the phone to Al Hampel in his hotel room in Los Angeles. It wasn't *Stardust*, but it was just as memorable to me.

I got the script for the next *Jack Benny* TV show about three weeks before taping in Los Angeles. All I had to do was tailor a Jell-O commercial around the theme of the show so that viewers would stay tuned. That final segment had to be such a seamless transition from the main story line that the viewer would not anticipate the commercial that was coming. They were called integrated commercials or cast commercials. "A spoonful of sugar helps the medicine go down." Because General Foods owned the show, the agency was entitled to use Jack Benny, Dennis Day, Don Wilson, Rochester, and Phil Harris to deliver Jell-O commercials woven into the show's fabric. Creating those commercials became my specialty at Y&R. And that's how I came to find myself winging to LA to meet with Irving Fein, Jack's manager who had approval of the script.

I walk into a small office on La Cienega and wait a few minutes for Irving Fein. My legs are aquiver like the consistency of Jell-O itself. I introduce myself and hand Mr. Fein the script. All the while, I'm thinking, *If I have to fly back to NY without approval from the Benny people, I can go back to writing trade ads*. Fein looks at it over for what seem like the time it would take for the show to play out. Eventually, he nods, as if in approval, but says, "I don't think so, but I'll show it to Jack." He goes into a back room and brings Jack Benny out to meet me. We shake hands, and I'm thrilled to learn his handshake is as limpid as mine, only drier. "What do you think, Jack? I'm not sure," says Fein. The great Jack Benny, a comedian I adored from radio days on, says with a smile, "I like it. I'll do it. Nice going, kid." I admit to slipping a line from one of the old radio shows into the script. I described Jack's eyes as being Lake Louise blue. I could have flown home without the plane. From then on, I became the integrated or cast commercial writer for such shows as *Andy Griffith, Hogan's Heroes, I Love Lucy, Jack Benny, Roy Rogers, Bugs Bunny* (Chuck Jones), *Jean Arthur, Carol Channing*, all for General Foods' products: Jell-O Gelatin, Jell-O Pudding and Pie Filling, Dream Whip, Sanka, Post Cereals, Log Cabin, Tang. All cast commercials required me being on the set at the shoot. My home in LA, sometimes for weeks on end, was the fabulous Bel-Air hotel, which spoiled me for every other hotel in the world.

PART 21

No Buddy Can Eat Just One

PASSING THOUGHT: EVERY morning, millions of men get into a scrape with a phenomenon known as hysteresis. If you shave with a multibladed razor, you benefit from hysteresis. This is ably demonstrated in Gillette's Trac II commercials in the early '70s: as the first blade cuts the whisker, it also pulls it out for the second blade to slice it off and leave nothing but smooth skin. So effective was this animated demonstration, research showed that shavers actually visualized the process as they were shaving. Trac II and hysteresis were so successful. Gillette, ever alert to product improvements and company profits, soon followed up with Mach 3 (three blades) and now Fusion with four blades. But since hysteresis proved that two blades provided the world's best shave, why the extra blades, which are nothing more than sluggards? Because men are willing to pay more for the perception of an even-closer shave. As if that wasn't enough, now Gillette sticks an AA battery in the handle of the razor and gets even more money for the tingle provided with Mach 3 Power and Fusion Power razors and blades. You get a hand vibrator and a pleasant buzz but provably no better shave than you get with the original Trac II. It seems that men are not averse to paying more money for an even-closer shave, perceived or imagined, in a process Gillette has termed "face validity."

When the Friendly Lion, a.k.a. Bert Lahr, passed away, Y&R and FritoLay faced a serious dilemma. Lay's Potato Chip commercials, starring Bert Lahr were working so well; i.e., selling so many potato chips. The challenge was to keep the momentum while finding a replacement for Lahr. I never thought the Lahr spots were that good, but the likeability of Bert Lahr prevailed, and the advertisement became among the most popular of the time. Buddy Hackett as a replacement for the inimitable Lahr was near or at the top of every decision maker on the FritoLay account, including myself who had Hackett as first choice. With my experience writing cast commercials for many of TV's leading shows, I became the designated front man for the Buddy Hackett project. My first assignment was to get FritoLay to sign on for Hackett at the then-generous fee of three thousand dollars for one year's use of Buddy Hackett for advertising in any or all media. It was not the easiest sale I ever had to make. The decision makers in Dallas knew Hackett from his many appearances on *Ed Sullivan* and *Johnny Carson*. His Chinese waiter bit remains a classic comedic gem. He had also starred in Disney's *Love Bug*. He was not unknown to the client, yet they had qualms about Hackett's reputed intractability and his history of blue material in his Vegas act. I negotiated the contract for Buddy with his manager and lawyer, Paul Sherman, who was to become a good friend. He was not the typical Hollywood barracuda. While extracting every advantage for his client, he was also fair and square with me. Paul Sherman, Wally Sheft, Buddy's accountant, and Joe Kelman, a close friend from Chicago, were known as the Hack Pack. As Buddy Hackett's representative for advertising, I automatically qualified for membership in the Hack Pack. It was like getting a private pass to the exciting world of show business topped by the unique privilege of hanging out with Hackett in Las Vegas every time he appeared in Sin City, which was quite often.

With his roly-poly girth and a mouth that worked only out of one corner, Buddy Hackett had a head start on funny. Once, when he was playing the lounge at the Sahara Hotel, Don Rickles saw Buddy in the audience. "Hey, there's Buddy Hackett. Buddy, why don't you paint stripes on your ass and go as a beach ball." When you hung out with Buddy, as I eventually did, you had to marvel at his improvised brilliance. Not a joke teller per se, but a storyteller who drew inspiration from everyday events and ordinary people and came up with unimaginable twists that were hilarious. Buddy played Vegas a half-dozen times a year and sold out every performance. I would watch as he convulsed audiences. Many times women would reluctantly leave the room to relieve themselves. He delighted in breaking me up, which was constantly. No sooner did we go into production of Lay's Potato Chip commercials, starring Buddy Hackett, then I became a mediator as well as a creative director.

The client had settled on the words they deemed inviolate in every spot, "So light, so thin, so crisp, you can eat a million of 'em but nobody can eat just one." Buddy thought, *By the time you say all that crap, the commercial is over*. Where's the room for comedy? he would ask. Therein lay the dichotomy. The client insisted on the sell. Buddy was playing for laughs, at the expense of the sell, if he had his way. And in the middle was Al Hampel. Every script I brought to Buddy created a tug, sell words or comedy. If I had not endeared myself to Buddy Hackett early in our relationship, he would have thrown me out on my ass. Deep down, he knew I was right. The obvious solution was compromise. With a soft-spoken argument for an approach that featured both humor and sell, I eventually convinced the giant among comedians of the day to do it my way, shortchanging neither Lay's nor Buddy. Often I couldn't believe I was telling Buddy Hackett how to be funny in the context of delivering the selling idea. He bought my act, and we went on to produce dozens of commercials and had a lot of fun in the process.

After a while, Buddy caught the hang of the compromise, and he began to improvise funny spots that did not sacrifice those precious words, "So light, so thin, so crisp, you can eat a million of 'em but nobody can eat just one." He even went as far as delivering a half-dozen improvised commercials when only one was scheduled for production.

We had a happy client in Dallas. Best of all, the commercials were so successful (sales were at an all-time high) that FritoLay renewed Buddy's contract for another year at an increased fee. At one of Buddy's shows at the Sahara Hotel in Vegas, there was a bag of Lay's imprinted with "No Buddy Can East Just One" at every table, and in the middle of his act, Buddy introduced me to the audience as the creator of the campaign. I stood to a rousing ovation in a packed showroom in Vegas. Can any other advertising copywriter make that claim? In the meantime, back at Y&R, I had been promoted to senior vice president and copy chief, the head of a department of hugely talented copywriters, most of whom were older than I was. I was in my midthirties and the youngest ever to have held the job of copy chief of Y&R. My dream of making it to Madison Avenue was realized in a fashion I could never have envisioned, a job with a title, which in those days represented one of the most highly respected positions in the world's most creative industry.

But alas, the Buddy Hackett saga came to an ignominious end. I had arranged to have Buddy perform at a Pepsi bottlers annual meeting in Texas. He put on a hell of a show. Delivering some of his raunchiest material, the bottlers laughed hysterically and gave Buddy a long standing ovation. Afterward, I had Buddy meet Don Kendall, Pepsi Cola's CEO (Pepsi owned FritoLay). The two exchanged pleasantries, but then Kendall said something to the effect that he enjoyed Buddy's work in the Lay's commercials, adding a *but*, "In some of those spots, I couldn't make out what you were saying." There was a long pause while I went numb, and Buddy got a faraway look in his eye. I knew what was coming. Hackett replied, "Hey, mister, I don't know what the fuck you're talking about now." Some weeks later, Buddy was on *Johnny Carson* when he revealed he was no longer working for Lay's Potato Chips. "Those chips didn't taste good. I didn't like them." Carson said, "But, Buddy, you been telling me for years how great those chips were, and nobody can eat just one. How come you've been hawking them for so long?" "Hey, John, for what they were paying me, I would eat dog shit." Buddy retained his record as the most bleeped guest ever on the *Johnny Carson* show.

PART 22

People Who Never Thought They'd Meet Al Hampel

I WAS AT THE pool one late August afternoon when I got a phone call from Buddy. "Hey, Al, a friend of mine wants to see the show tonight, but she's alone, and she would like an escort to sit with her." "Of course, I'll go. The first show?"

"Alvin, all you gotta do is tell the maître d', and he'll show you to the table, ringside. You will like her, she is a nice person."

I get to the showroom promptly at eight, hand the captain a ten-dollar chip, and I'm led to the table where an attractive blonde in a white sequined off-the-shoulder dress awaits. The early arrivals for Buddy's first show around ringside now shift their gaze from her to "Who's the lucky guy?" She extends her hand. "Hi, I'm Phyllis McGuire. You must be Al." Phyllis McGuire of the McGuire sisters who I used to see on the *Arthur Godfrey* show? Can this be Phyllis McGuire, the girlfriend of mobster Sam Giancana? And I'm supposed to watch the show?

It turned out to be a wonderful evening. She was delightful, and we both laughed until it hurt. When it was over, I walked Phyllis McGuire through the casino to her car, amid stares and whistles from the one-armed bandit crowd. She did not offer, "I'd like to see you again," and I did not say, "Can I have your phone number?" All I could think of as I walked back, *I had a date with the mistress of Sam Giancana, one of the most ruthless of mob bosses. And I lived to tell about it.* Later when I went backstage to visit Buddy, I said, "She was great. Who you got for me tomorrow night, Mrs. John Gotti?"

One night, I accompanied Buddy to a testimonial dinner for Vin Scully, the famed voice of the Los Angeles Dodgers and a legend in LA. Buddy was one of the speakers and a laugh riot as usual. As the dinner broke up, Buddy cornered Cary Grant walking off the dais, found me in the audience, and steered the rather reclusive actor to meet Alvin Hampel. I shook his hand, which was even clammier than mine. "It's a pleasure, Mr. Grant, Gary, I'm sorry, Cary." In the middle of one of the most stuttering, most nervous responses to meeting one of the all-time greats, Buddy nudges me and says, "Cary, not Harry, you schmuck." Cary Grant doubled over laughing. The Sahara Hotel's house for its star performers was a way station for anyone visiting or performing at other Vegas hotels. When Sean Connery dropped by for a round of golf with Buddy, I was invited to walk the course with them. In addition to watching a couple of duffers, I witnessed an Olympian event of wisecrack and expletive hurling, expectedly from Buddy, but surprisingly from the urbane Mr. Connery. Apparently, the Scots also invented the cant that facilitated the exciting and exacting new game of golf. It was great fun to watch 007 confront a terrorist more sinister than Odd Job or Goldfinger. Buddy Hackett messed up every one of Sean Connery's swings with a weapon 007 could not defuse. He made Connery laugh. Much of Buddy's take on golf is recounted in the book he wrote, *The Truth About Golf and Other Lies*.

I got in the car, and we were off on a magical mystery drive. I don't ask. Hackett doesn't tell. We stop at a modest ranch (if there are any in Beverly Hills), and the woman working in the kitchen bids us a warm welcome then ushers into the den. I sit in big leather chair, look around at the many artifacts and photos that should have been a clue to who lived here. There weren't. In just a few minutes, a smiling hulk of a man shuffles in and greets us with clicking and sucking sounds that are uniquely this man's signature. When I come to, I am being introduced to Jonathan Winters. Who is going to believe this? I have been turned into an audience of one sitting between two of the most inventive comedic minds who waste no time beginning to *shpritz* (the term that describes two or more comedians throwing laugh lines at each other in a can-you-top this fashion). Sensing they had a pigeon for an audience, these two guys put on a show for my benefit. That hour in the home of a true legend became one the most memorable of my life. Imagine actually meeting Maude Frickert.

PART 23

Countdown to Liftoff

MEANWHILE, BACK AT Y&R, I was on a mission to run the table, from sales promotion writer to copywriter, sharing a small office with another copywriter, then on to copy supervisor and my own office plus a secretary. What a wonderful partner came my way in the person of a recent Manhattanville College grad named Maura Kavanagh. Tall, blond, blue eyed, and very bright, Maura not only typed my copy, she edited it too. I hit the Irish sweepstakes. Maura remains a friend of the Hampel family to this day. Next came a giant step up to associate creative director and ultimate creative responsibility for a half-dozen important accounts. My office space grew as large as the office of the copy department head who first interviewed me. It had two gigantic windows and came with the privilege of picking out my own furnishings. It was here where the legendary yellow paisley sofa, which drew more visitors to my office just to glimpse it, made its debut. Someone said, "Wow, you could throw up on it, and no one would know the difference." Someone once did. With associate creative director came the mantle of vice president of the company. Imagine, the nebbish from Twenty-Third Street, a VP of Young & Rubicam, the paragon of the craft of advertising, the engine of American business. When I excitedly phoned my dad to give him the news of my promotion, he said "*Mazel tov*. How old is the president?"

Navigating the talent-laden layers in the highly structured creative department at Y&R was no cakewalk. After all, I could not leap tall buildings or fly faster than jet airplanes or skip the hierarchy of the agency's organization even though I was once referred to as "Super Jew" in a pejorative way by a Texaco client at another ad agency. When I arrived at Y&R in 1957, it didn't take long for me to size up the landscape. Now the nebbish from Twenty-Third Street in Paterson, New Jersey, was in the big leagues, like a rookie shortstop from the minors on his first day on a major league team roster. What will it take to shine in this environment among copywriting stars whose award-winning print ads and TV reels make my meager output look like typical catalog copy?

Alan Jay Lerner of the musical writing team of Lerner and Loewe was once asked why so much time elapsed between writing of his shows. "It's not that I'm slow to write. I'm just quick to throw out." (Lerner was married eight times.) I subscribed to Lerner's method. In fact, I became a fanatic. For every headline I ever wrote, I rejected dozens and dozens. I knew what I was after, and I was never satisfied until I reached that "aha" moment. Every assignment became a challenge on which my reputation rested. So I chased the winning solution while at home, during the commute, while on long walks and doing chores around the house, before bed, and upon waking. Chasing perfection can drive a person crazy. My wife will attest that it did. There was always a better headline around the corner. The idea was to keep going until you found it. Years later, at another ad agency, I distributed buttons in the form of a Stop sign but with the word "Don't" superimposed on top. I still have a limited supply, so if you want one, e-mail me, alhamp@aol.com.

Early on, I identified what I was after. I worked to create the kind of advertising that would attract me and that I would remember. That genre is best summed up in the word "unexpected." I think people like surprises in advertising, just as they do the unexpected endings of stories by O. Henry, Poe, Roald Dahl, and films by Hitchcock. Most advertising is so boring; an unexpected approach stops the reader or viewer and contributes to memorability. And that's why I'm also a great believer of *humor* in advertising. The punch line of a joke is the perfect example of the unexpected.

A case in point: George Burns was asked, "What was your worst sexual experience?" Burns replied, "Terrific." The most popular and most memorable TV commercials are almost always the humorous ones. Searching for a headline for a Jell-O Pudding ad, the strategy of which was Jell-O's superior texture or smoothness, I must have filled two pages of possible captions before finally settling on "Jell-O Believes You've Taken Enough Lumps in Your Life." The line ran over a scrumptious Irving Penn photo of a dish of Jell-O Pudding. The ad was an award winner. It has been said, "Success is a matter of luck, tenacity, attitude, and talent. The loss of any one can sink you. But if you have all four, success is assured."

I could influence the latter three, and I did. But luck? How do you get lucky? You have it, or you don't. Luck came to me when I was assigned to General Foods and particularly its flagship brand, Jell-O Gelatin. It was one of Y&R's oldest and most carefully nurtured accounts. My first job for Jell-O began when I subbed for an ailing copywriter and wrote a cast or integrated commercial for the *Jack Benny* show. It featured the stars of the show and appeared to be a continuation of the story line but was really a pitch for Jell-O Gelatin's new fresh fruit flavors woven seamlessly into the show's theme.

Sometimes the Benny writers would help polish my scripts. The job of crafting General Foods commercials for some of the most popular TV sitcoms of the day became my stock in trade. I was forever winging off to LA to oversee my General Foods spots as they were produced at such studios as Desilu and Warner Bros. I remember kidding around with five-year-old Ron Howard, while as Opie, he waited for his next scene on the *Andy Griffith Show*. The kid grew to be one of Hollywood's legendary award-winning directors. These were undoubtedly exciting times as I fancied myself a TV sitcom scriptwriter for the shows I would watch on my twelve-inch DuPont TV in our apartment back home in Paterson. Who'd have thought that the nebbish from Twenty-Third Street would make it in show business? Wasn't I producing miniature thirty—and sixty-second movies that were seen by more people than many feature films?

To those who knew me best, I was in the process of leaving my humility on the doorstep and morphing from a nebbish to a *gonse k'nocker* (a big deal). It didn't hurt to have a patron in a high post at Y&R. Mine was Dermott McCarthy, a big lovable Irishman who was copy chief of the agency. He dug my copy and always matched my style with accounts that appreciated the unexpected. We took memorable trips to the West Coast together. LA was Dermott's hometown. The plane would no sooner land, then Dermott would schlep me to one of his old haunts, a neighborhood bar where he knew every bartender and most of the patrons. One time, he took me to lunch at a convent where his sister was a nun in residence. It was okay, I was wearing a mezuzah at the time. Dermott loved his martinis. Try as he did, he could not convert this Manischewitz drinker. When he and Dorothy flew out together to meet me in LA, he almost made a *shikker* (drunk) out of my wife during the flight. Martinis before and during were Dermott's antidote for fear of flying. The flight attendants who served him became his friends, and those flights turned into parties in the sky. One flight attendant became Dermott's secretary. Dermott McCarthy was the first one to recommend me to replace him as copy chief of the agency when he went off to become the creative director of the European offices.

PART 24

Among My Souvenirs

UNTIL I ARRIVED at Y&R, I had never written a TV commercial. Of necessity, I was strictly a writer of print advertising. Print presented a neat package of headline, subheadline, an illustration designed to capture the attention of the reader, body copy where most of the sell took place, and a logo and theme line at the ad bottom that identified the sponsor. Print advertising filled the sample book that helped get me the job at Y&R. At the time, TV commercials, while not in their infancy, were still black and white and sixty seconds in length and on a path to overtake print as the dominant advertising medium of many large advertisers. The idea of creating TV spots intimidated me. What is this stuff: dissolve, match dissolve, cut, CU and ECU, super? I didn't understand this lingo, so how would I ever create commercials containing those production directions?

On the verge of panic, a terrific veteran copywriter named Bob Higbee took me aside and told me to forget the technical mumbo jumbo and to just write down how I visualized the commercial and the words that went with it. That good advice freed me up to jump into TV commercials and create some pretty good ones over the years. But I never lost my love of print even as it seems to be on a course to oblivion. Following are some of the highlights of my years at Y&R. Most advertising is the result of teamwork. You might get the initial idea for an ad, but it cannot be produced in a vacuum. A team of assorted specialists contribute to the finished ad: art directors, designers, photographers, actors, directors, producers, editors, and the crews who work on commercials. It takes almost as many people to film a TV commercial as it does to produce a feature film.

As mentioned previously, Jell-O offered the opportunity to produce imaginative, eye-catching work that became a passport to success and promotion at Y&R. I made the most of the opportunity. Jell-O Cheesecake, the no-bake cheesecake. Simple setup. Husband and wife. And two of the most talented actors in film and theater: Louise Lasser, famous for the series *Mary Hartman, Mary Hartman,* and Josh Shelly, a veteran featured player in Hollywood, who had no lines in this commercial but just continued to eat and enjoy the cheesecake, oblivious to his wife's delivery of the copy points. Finally getting no response to her question, "Do you like it?" She self-answers it with a last line, "He likes it." A simple spot that won a CLIO, presented at the awards ceremony by Woody Allen, married to Louise Lasser at the time. A campaign for Jell-O Pudding and Pie Filling featuring Paul Lynde as the presenter. Lynde, who was gay, was not an easy sale to the uptight, conservative culture at General Foods. Lynde's fey style turned the commercials into comic gems, but not at the expense of the selling points. Such lines as, "If I'm not telling you the truth my nose will grow longer" and interacting with a horse at a farm, "Treacherous beast," delivered by Paul Lynde made people laugh as much as they did when he responded to loaded questions on the popular show, *Hollywood Squares.* Turned out that the Lynde commercials got the highest memorability scores in copy testing and sold a lot of Jell-O Pudding and Pie Filling. Only then did General Foods retain him for another season.

"There's Always Room for Jell-O" was one of the most renowned of all Jell-O campaigns. The ads featured ethnic family feasts: Italian, Jewish, Greek, etc. These were large cast commercials showing guests enjoying the various courses, followed at the end of the meal by the only desert there was room for, *Jell-O.* This campaign was a classic example of product as hero and a cinch winner of the CLIO Awards for best of package goods commercials.

"Vote For Your Favorite Jell-O Flavor in the GREAT BIG JELL-O ELECTION." Each flavor had its campaign slogan displayed in a two-page rendering of campaigners parading with signs touting their favorites. The big ad ran in Sunday magazine sections. Buttons featuring the slogans were distributed nationwide, "Sweet on Strawberry," "I'm for Lime," "Ape for Grape," "Cheers for Cherry," "Lemon's my Squeeze," "Orange has the Juice," "Nothing to buy." All you had to do was select your favorite on the coupon in the ad. Hundreds of thousands voted. Strawberry won in a landslide. This idea was way ahead of its time. It was ideally suited to be a promotion on the Internet many years later. Cherry demanded a recount.

No sooner did General Foods sign with Warner Bros. for the use of Bugs Bunny as spokesman for Tang, the instant breakfast drink, then I headed west to meet with Chuck Jones. From the forward to *Chuck Amuck: The Life and Times of an Animated Cartoonist*, Steven Spielberg wrote, "With the creation of Pepe LePew, Coyote, and Road Runner and as part of the team that created Daffy Duck, Porky Pig, and directed over fifty Bugs Bunny cartoons, Chuck broke away from those sweet preschool characters to whom Walt Disney had given eternal life." It did not soothe my nerves to know I would be working with the king of animated cartoonists. I discussed my idea for the commercial with Jones in his office. I envisioned Bugs Bunny in "Tangrila." He sparked at the idea, and I silently sighed a "whew." We went off to the Warner Bros. commissary for lunch, and Jones sketched the whole thing out on a place mat, which I now have framed on my wall at home. As newcomers to the Tang account, the creative team took a field trip to Battle Creek, Michigan, to see how Tang was produced. The process was little more than a variety of powders moved from vats to a jar. For sanitary reasons, we all had to don white paper hats. I thought, *If a hair ever got into Tang, it would be the only natural ingredient in it.*

Switching to print, I enjoyed an incredible run of Gulf advertising one three-month period. For Gulfspray, an insecticide, the page was blank except for one dead bug on its back on the bottom and the line, "Not Everyone Benefits From Gulf Research." A Whitney Darrow Jr. cartoon depicting two kids talking through empty Gulf Oil cans connected by string and the line, "The Best Way an Oil Company Talks to Its Customers is Through Its Products." The photo showed the contents of a woman's handbag strewn about the page and a Gulf credit card prominently featured. The line, "A Woman Doesn't Get Very Far Without Certain Basic Necessities." Harry MacMahan who wrote a column for Advertising Age titled "The Month's Ten Best" included each of the above ads three months in a row.

PART 25

The Carol Channing Show

IF YOU WANTED to cast someone to oversee the General Foods shows for which Y&R was agency of record, you couldn't do better than Bud Barry. Tall, handsome, with white hair atop a ruddy complexion and a hint of an Irish brogue. Charismatic Bud Barry was most importantly a salesman. He could sell Hershey's bars to the Mars brothers. Salesmanship was the essential skill necessary to negotiate with the assorted Hollywood types that Bud dealt with on behalf of General Foods. Only a man with Bud Barry's experience and temperament could wheedle concessions from that crowd. Internally, Barry ran his department with little slack for ineptitude. The only time his face would turn more florid than usual was when he summoned his minions to his office for a grilling. "Now, Colgan, what were you supposed to do that you didn't?" And a shaky Colgan Shlank would spill his kishkes (guts) out, even confess to the seven deadly sins to avoid the wrath of a Bud Barry who thought you were holding out on him. Still the TV honchos on the West Coast and the sitcom's performers loved Bud Barry. I remember a meeting with George Burns, and when Burns learned that I was from Y&R, he immediately asked about Bud Barry. "Bud has had some health issues," I replied. "In and out of the hospital." Why I followed up with, "His wife died," I don't know. But in the context in which I blurted the sad news, George Burns laughed out loud. He could laugh; he was in his nineties. And that's how I made George Burns laugh.

Incidentally, Florence, Bud's wonderful wife, ran a renowned resale shop called Encore where some of New York's most famous socialites turned in their schmattes (hardly ever worn frocks) for immediate cash. My wife, Dorothy, became friendly with Florence and was let in on a collector's item, a Valentino coat owned by Jackie Onassis. Florence confided to Dorothy that Jackie was a ferocious *hondler* (bargainer), often asking more for her worn clothes than they were worth. Dorothy bought the coat and would trot it out for all her friends to see. It was a lovely A-line apricot-colored garment. Dorothy treasured the memento though she rarely wore it. Eventually it disappeared from her wardrobe.

One day, I got a call from Bud Barry asking me to come to his office for an important meeting. What could Bud want to see me about? Not one of those infamous interrogations. I don't even work for the guy. "Chum [a greeting borrowed from Walter Bunker, Bud's West Coast representative and a legend in radio and TV circles on the coast], I got a big one for you," said Barry, jumping up excitedly from behind his desk. "I just bought Carol Channing for General Foods. I got Charles Lowe, Channing's husband, to throw in the lady to do commercials on the show." Since Carol Channing had never done commercials, this was a major concession and only the inimitable Bud Barry could swing it. "Here's what I need from you, Mr. Hampel. I want you to tell me how to use Carol Channing in five or six commercials and then write them so they will be acceptable to her and Mr. Lowe and most of all to General Foods. I know you're going to love this. I need them by Tuesday morning for a presentation to the client for approval." It was then Friday afternoon when Bud Barry was laying this on me. He's got to be kidding. "I've got all that time? Hell, I could write the whole show in that time," trying to make a nervous joke out of a next-to-impossible request. *Here's where I go on my ass* was all that I could think of. "Brother Hampel, I'm going to put you up in a suite in the Plaza Hotel for the weekend, and you can order anything you want from room service. Send out for stuff if you need it. Bring all your writing gear, and give me the best you got. This'll make you famous. Hell, I'll even supply the girls. Whaddya like, blondes, redheads, brunettes, what other colors they come in? You name it, you got it."

I'd be lying if I said I didn't consider Bud Barry's offer. But my saner head prevailed, and I trudged across town and caught a bus to our modest little home and my wife and kids in Wayne, New Jersey. And for one whole weekend, I played husband and daddy, while never being uninvolved with Carol Channing. Usually, I put aside the first idea that comes to mind. That would be in keeping with the theory of "Don't Stop," which I always encouraged my creative people to observe. Try some more. There might be a better idea around the corner. But in this case, I violated my own tradition. I felt so strongly about the first idea that popped into my head that Saturday morning that I stopped. "That's it." So I had the rest of the weekend to write the copy for Carol Channing and others she would interact with if my idea was accepted. It had to be approved by Barry, Ed Ebel, the head man at General Foods, Charles Lowe, Carol's husband and manager, Carol Channing, the producer and writers of the show, and who knows, assorted others. This was a gauntlet that could chip away, even kill my idea. What if they all didn't like it? You never stop fretting till the finished product is in the can, meaning produced and ready for airing. The next time I heard from Bud was a phone call on a Wednesday afternoon from White Plains, the headquarters of General Foods. "Brother Hampel, pack your bags. You're off to meet with Hello Dolly. See you next week at the Bel-Air hotel." So began one of the most magical periods of my show business career.

The following are excerpts from a review in the *Hollywood Daily Variety* of Monday, February 21, 1966: "AN EVENING WITH CAROL CHANNING," Carol Channing's first TV special was an unmitigated disappointment. Those who masterminded didn't appear to know how to transfer the gifted Miss Channing's many talents of song and mimicry to the small screen, and the result was a generally vapid and unfunny show. There was a cloying approach throughout most of the tint hour. It seemed as though those in charge theorized viewers wouldn't understand Miss Channing's great routines and her wonderful ability to mime, so they steered her into a cornfield instead, etc., etc . . . Producer-director was Bud Yorkin. Writers were Hal Goodman, Al Gordon and Sheldon Keller. Choreo by Hermes Pan was undistinguished. INTEGRATED BLURBS IN WHICH MISS CHANNING APPEARED WITH ANDY GRIFFITH, JIM NABORS, EVA GABOR, EDDIE ALBERT AND HOGAN'S HEROES GANG—ALL SPONSORED BY GENERAL FOODS—WERE THE MOST INVENTIVE, INGENIOUS AND AMUSING PART OF THE SPEC. WHOEVER PRODUCED THESE SHOULD HAVE PRODUCED THE SHOW."

PART 26

The Speech

THERE'S A LIFE changer in every life. Sometimes called a turning point, it might be a new job, a promotion, a chance meeting, a wedding, a journey, the lottery—mine was a speech.

When invited to address the creative session of the annual 4A's meeting (American Association of Advertising Agencies) at the Greenbrier hotel, one of the plushest resorts in America, my immediate reaction was twofold. I was pumped about the prestigious platform and petrified of the daunting task of mounting and delivering a knockout talk to an audience of top ad executives.

I quote from a recent book, *Confessions of a Public Speaker* by Scott Berkun: "Public speaking is one of our greatest fears. More frightening than snakes, spiders or heights. The terror of exposure and humiliation in front of others—of flubbing one's lines or saying the wrong thing or being plain boring."

Before this invitation, the closest I had come to speaking in public was when I presented my work in client meetings. That hardly qualified me for the gig to come. I felt like an up-and-coming young entertainer who was suddenly thrust onto the big stage before paying his or her dues as a lounge act. Still, I was thrilled at the opportunity.

The speech was scheduled for April 27, 1968, so I had about a month to write, rewrite, rehearse, add and subtract, and ultimately submit the script to top Y&R brass who insisted on vetting the speech to make sure I wasn't alienating any of our clients. They went pretty easy with the red pencil, but they did censor some funny lines, which they didn't get. I went along thinking, what the heck, when I'm up there I can stick to the original script, and there will be nothing they could do about it. It was customary for the agency to submit the script to the press ahead of time to get maximum publicity. The title of the speech was "Losing Money the Creative Way or Watch Out for Clients in Pleated Pants."

I felt it was time to shine a light on the inanities that were making creative departments ripe for lampooning. I had lots of material to work with. The people at the 4A's who were in charge of the conference kept asking me about the commercials I intended to show during my talk. How long was the reel? How long the talk? It seemed every other speaker in the creative slot showed slews of their best commercials, which almost always guaranteed good audience response. There was stunned disbelief when they learned I was going sans film. Every time they asked, "Are you sure?" they made me more nervous.

I was scheduled to speak Saturday morning. Wednesday of that week, I hitched a ride on a charter flight headed directly to White Sulphur Springs, West Virginia, the home of the Greenbrier hotel. It was the worst of flights. It was the best of flights. We took off in the kind of weather that brought New Orleans to its knees. Hey, weren't we supposed to fly *over* the George Washington Bridge? You couldn't tell my stomach we were not on the Cyclone in Coney Island. How did I ever wind up in this de Havilland Otter, getting tossed around with a bunch of golfers passing as ad men and magazine and newspaper publishers and my interest in golf was occasionally watching it on TV. But there's always a bright side: if this thing goes down, I won't have to make that f—ing speech. About twenty minutes into the flight, there came an announcement from the flight deck, "Ladies and gentlemen, we will be making an emergency stop in Trenton to remove someone who has taken sick."

It was the pilot. Soon, we were treated to a rare sight, the incapacitated pilot, ashen-faced, held up by two crew members, and literally dragged off the airplane. It didn't take long for a replacement pilot to come aboard. He was a tall, nice-looking young man dressed in a sweater and holding a stack of rolled-up maps under his arm. Looking around the plane, he innocently asked the passengers, "Is this flight going to South Carolina?" There would be no respite from worry.

After revealing our destination to the pilot, the flight proceeded south without further incident. But just as were about to land in White Sulphur Springs, West Virginia, an idea hit me. In the story of this crazy flight, I'd been handed a funny new opening to my speech. And that's how the worst of flights became the best of flights.

As soon as I checked in, I made a reservation to return by train. I had time to kill before Saturday morning, so I hiked the hills surrounding the beautiful Greenbrier, all the while going over the lines and practicing my timing. During my walk, I met one veteran of 4A meetings who dropped this little gem on me: "Hey, kiddo, if the sun is shining Saturday, they'll all be out there getting in their last day of golf. And you're going to be talking to a lovely bunch of seats."

Friday night was for the traditional black tie gala—lots of good food and drink plus celebrity entertainment and dancing. Around midnight, as Ed Bond, CEO of Y&R, and I were walking to the elevator, we encountered Phil Dougherty. Bond grabs Phil, pulls me over, and introduces me to the legendary *NY Times* advertising news columnist. "Al is the creative speaker tomorrow morning. I believe you have a copy of his speech." Phil Dougherty, read by everyone in advertising, had the power to affect your career by what he wrote about you. This evening, Phil barely mustered the power to stand. He waves and mumbles, incapable of responding, except, "You call that piece of crap a speech." "Good night, Phil. It was nice meeting you."

That night, the eve before the big speech, was not the most restful night I ever spent. At one point, I even considered attacking the minibar in my room. No, I had just been a victim of the ravages of alcohol. I had to be alert and ready the next morning. I settled for a frozen Milky Way. I know what he's going to write, "Hampel winds up conference and his career."

I awoke the next morning to a pouring rain. Apparently, the good Lord wanted me to speak to a full house. As the 9:30 AM deadline approached, I found myself sitting, totally unnerved, on stage, watching some 800 moaning, groaning golfers and assorted other weekend athletes stream into the auditorium without a clue of what to expect. They had nowhere else to go.

Paraphrasing the headline on David Ogilvy's famous Rolls-Royce ad, "The loudest sound you could hear was the clop, clop, clop of my heart." After a lavish introduction by Ed Bond, I approached the lectern with the apprehension of a golfer on the first tee and let it roll. I pulled out a line I saved for just such an occasion:

"Of all the introductions I've ever had, that is by far the most recent." And just like that, I had my first laugh. The ice was broken.

My hunch was right. The story of the flight from hell proved to be a major laugh getter. Then into the body of the speech skewering the absurdities of creativity in advertising, I was interrupted by laughter dozens of times. The longer I spoke, the more I thought, *I'm actually enjoying this.*

There was no shortage of targets to goof on: awards, meetings, plan boards, difficult clients, backup campaigns, commercial testing, creative teams, location shoots, production costs, piggyback commercials, and client attire. At one point I discussed the advantages of nudity. I asked the audience to imagine that they are all attending a wedding in the nude. I asked them to visualize the entire congregation in the nude. At the proper time, the minister questions the young bride-to-be, "Do you take this man to be your lawful wedded husband?" She slowly studies the room and randomly points into the crowd. "No, I think I take that one over there." The house came down. When the speech was over, I walked—make that floated—to the back of the auditorium to a standing ovation, lots of handshakes, dozens of business cards, and two job offers. I had never experienced anything like that high.

In Monday morning's *New York Times*, Phil Dougherty wrote: "Al Hampel, copy chief of Y&R. closed the 4A's Conference with a funny romp through the inanities of the ad business. He had the audience laughing and nodding in agreement with his barbs. Al Hampel has a future as a stand-up comedian."

ABOUT THE AUTHOR:

AS A YOUNGSTER in Paterson, N.J., Al Hampel worked part time as a salesman in men's clothing stores. Concurrently he wrote a column for his school newspaper. Looking ahead he decided there was one career that combined both of his favorite pastimes, selling and writing. The choice was obvious. He would be an advertising copywriter.

After a series of copywriting jobs in small ad agencies and companies around New Jersey, the ladder led to a copywriting job at Young & Rubicam, one of Madison Avenue's premier advertising agencies. Eventually he became copy chief, head of all copy in the agency. As copy chief, Hampel was able to write and influence some of advertising's most notable ad campaigns, including Jell-O, Lay's Potato Chips, Beautyrest, J&J, Piel's Beer, Eastern Airlines, Bulova, General Electric, Breck Hair Products, Remington Shavers etc.

After retiring from the ad business, Al Hampel taught a course in advertising copywriting at the University of Arizona.

He lives with his wife Dorothy in New York City.

INDEX

A

advertising, 48
 business-to-business, 63
Advertising Age, 81
AIG (American Insurance Group), 55
Allen, Woody, 45, 80
Allies, 32
American Association of Advertising Agencies, 85–88
Amicis, 18, 20
Amos Parrish and Co., 52–54
Andy Griffith Show, 68, 77, 84
Anna (Alvin's aunt), 22–23
Anton, Mark, 51
Arthur Godfrey show, 73
Aunt Selma (Alvin's aunt), 11–12
Automat, 23
Avis, 43
Axis, 32

B

Band-Aids, 60
Bates, Ted, 58
Beacon, 42
Beautyrest, 60, 65–66

Belafonte, Harry, 61
Bel-Air hotel, 68, 84
Benny, Jack, 67–68, 77
Berkun, Scott
 Confessions of a Public Speaker, 85
Berle, Milton, 45
Bernbach, Bill, 43
Betty Robbins School of Dance, 46
Bomba the Jungle Boy series, 16
Bond, Ed, 87
Bond, Ward, 61
Booz Allen Hamilton, 58
Borden's Elsie commercial, 60
Boston Red Sox, 14, 21, 49, 67
Botany Mills, 45
Breck, 60
Brickman's hotel, 45
Brooks, Mel, 45
Bubbe (Alvin's maternal grandmother), 14–15
Bugs Bunny (cartoon character), 81
Bugs Bunny (show), 68
Bunker, Walter, 83
Burdines, 52
Burns, George, 2, 76, 82
Bush, George H. W., 36
Buttons, Red, 45

C

Cadillac, 43
Camp Elliot, 40
Carlin, George, 53
Carmichael, Hoagy, 67
Carol Channing Show, 68, 82, 84
Carson Pirie Scott, 52
Catskills, 44–45
Channing, Carol, 83–84
Charmin, 55
Chivas Regal, 43
Chrysler, 55, 60–61
Chuck Amuck: The Life and Times of an Animated Cartoonist (Jones), 81
Clapton, Eric, 62
Clark, Petula, 61
Clinton, Bill, 44
Clinton, Hillary, 49
CLIO Awards, 80
Coke, 17
Colliers, 16
commercials, integrated/cast, 67
Concord hotel, 45
Coney Island, 12, 86
Confessions of a Public Speaker (Berkun), 85
Connery, Sean, 74
Convoy, 40
Cooper, James Fenimore, 16
copywriting, 48, 65
Corning, 55
Coyote, 81
Crisp, Coco, 67
Criterion, 42
Crompton & Knowles, 7

D

Daffy Duck, 81
Dahl, Roald, 76
Damoff's, 44
Darrow, Whitney, Jr., 81
Dartmouth College, 59
Day, Dennis, 67
DDB (Doyle Dane Bernbach), 42–43
Desilu, 77
Disney, Walt, 81
Doby, Larry, 29
Dougherty, Phil, 87–88
Drackett company, 61
Dream Whip, 68

E

Ebel, Ed, 84
Eberly, Bob, 32
Ed Sullivan show, 70
Eighteenth Street Raiders, 18
Eisenhower, Dwight David, 59
EL AL Airlines, 43
Empire State Building, 22, 55–56
Encore, 82
Erie Railroad station, 22
Excedrin, 60

F

Falstaff (beer), 40
Fitzgibbon, Bernice, 49
Florence (Alvin's cousin), 11–12
Florence (Bud Barry's wife), 82
Foley's, 52
Foote Cone & Belding, 54

4A. *See* American Association of Advertising Agencies
Frede, Joel, 56
Freed's grocery store, 9–10
Frickert, Maude, 74
FritoLay, 69–72
Froot Loops, 67

G

Galvin, Peggy, 50
GE (General Electric), 55, 60, 63
General Cigar, 60
General Foods, 67–68, 77, 80–84
Giancana, Sam, 73
Gigli, Ormond, 63
Gillette, 69
Gimbels, 49
Good Housekeeping, 34
Gordon, Cy, 42
Grant, Cary, 45, 74
Gray, Bobby, 52
Great Lakes Naval Training Station, 39
"Green Eyes," 32
Grey, Zane, 16
Grier, Jack, 66
Griesedieck, 40
Grossinger's hotel, 45
Gulf Oil, 63, 81
Gurantz, Herbert, 32

H

Hackett, Buddy, 30, 45, 69–74
  The Truth About Golf and Other Lies, 74
Hampel, Alvin
  childhood, 10, 13–24

family life, 7–11, 23–24
high school life, 29–30
war involvement, 36–40
advertising career, 16, 30, 41–42, 48–49, 52, 56, 62–63, 75–76
  Amos Parrish, 54
  Bamberger's, 48
  Benton & Bowles, 33
  Gordon-Pilling, 41–42, 48–49
  Hearst, 34
  Ralf Shockey and Associates, 55–56
  Suburban Propane News, 50
  Young & Rubicam, 58–59, 61–63, 65, 67–71, 75, 77, 79, 83
relationship with Ms. Betty, 46–47
married life, 24, 53, 58, 76–78, 82–83
speech, 85–88
Hampel, Alvin, Simmons Beautyrest commercials of, 65–66
Hampel, Daniel, 8, 58
Hampel, Dorothy, 53
Hampel, Leo, 7–8, 29
Harris, Phil, 67
Hecht's, 52
Helmar, 22
Herschel (Alvin's uncle), 14
Hershey's bars, 82
H&H Silk Co., 7–8
Higbee, Bob, 79
Hitchcock, Alfred, 76
Hitler, Adolf, 14, 29
Hogan's Heroes, 68
Hollywood Daily Variety, 84
Hollywood Squares, 80
Horowitz, Bull, 18
Howard, Ron, 77
Hudson's Bay, 52

I

I Love Lucy, 68
Irving, Fein, 68

J

Jack Benny show, 68, 77
Jean Arthur, 68
Jell-O, 56, 60, 67–68, 76–77, 79–80
Jersey Verein Club, 21
Jimmy Dorsey orchestra, 32
J&J baby products, 60
Johnny Carson show, 70, 72
Jones, Chuck, 68
   Chuck Amuck: The Life and Times of an Animated Cartoonist, 81

K

Kasen's Pants Store, 33–34
Kavanagh, Maura, 75
Kay's grocery store, 16–18
Kelman, Joe, 70
Kendall, Don, 72
Kennedy, John, 36
Kentucky Derby, 10
King, Alan, 45
Kutsher's hotel, 45

L

Larmon, Sig, 59
Lasser, Louise, 80
Lauren, Ralph, 8
Lay's Potato Chip, 69–70
Lerner, Alan Jay, 76
Lerner and Loewe, 76
Liberty, 16
Life Magazine, 63
Lifshitz, Ralph. *See* Lauren, Ralph
Lindbergh Hotel, 41, 44
Log Cabin, 68
London, Jack, 16
Los Angeles Dodgers, 74
Love Bug, 70
Lowe, Charles, 83–84
LP gas, 51
Luna Park, 12
Lynde, Paul, 80

M

MacMahan, Harry, 81
Macy's, 22, 49
Madison Avenue, New York, 41–42, 48, 52, 59, 65, 71
Mad Men, 61
Maeve, Erin, 67
Mandel (the other "Mondle" in Paterson), 21
Mars brothers, 82
Marshall Field's, 52
Mary Hartman, Mary Hartman, 80
Maytag, 61
McCain, John, 36
McCarthy, Dermott, 62, 77–78
McGuire, Phyllis, 73
McNally, Kevin, 61, 63

Meier & Frank, 52
Micronite Filter, 60
Modess, 60
Mondel, Louis. *See* Zeyde
Montecristo cigars, 51
Mr. Freed (grocery store owner), 9
Mr. Resnick (neighbor), 9
Mrs. Butterworth, 49, 67
Murray, Jan, 45

N

Nathan, Uncle, 11
Nathan's hot dogs, 11–12
New York Times, 48, 88

O

Obama, Barack, 49
O'Connell, Helen, 32
Ogilvy, David, 87
  Ogilvy on Advertising, 42
O. Henry, 76
Onassis, Jackie, 82

P

Pabst (beer), 40
Palmer, Arnold, 9, 63–64
Paterson, New Jersey, 7
Pearl Harbor, 32
Penn, Irving, 76
Pepe LePew, 81
Pepsi, 17, 71–72
P&G (Procter & Gamble), 55–56
Pilling, Ed, 42

Poe, Edgar Allan, 76
Porky Pig, 81
Post Cereals, 68

Q

Quackenbush's department store, 34

R

Rae, Murray, 52–53
Raft, George, 52
Ralf Shockey and Associates, 55–57
Reality in Advertising (Reeves), 42
Rely tampons (P&G), 56
Rickles, Don, 70
Road Runner, 81
Robbins, Betty, 46–47
Rochester (*Jack Benny* show actor), 67
Rocket (softball player), 19–20
Roma (Harry Gross's wife), 46
Roman, Freddy, 45
Roosevelt, Franklin Delano, 32
Rosser Reeves
  Reality in Advertising, 42
Rosten, Leo, 21
Roxyette, 46
Roy Rogers, 68
Rubicam, Harry, 58–59
Rubicam, Ray, 59
Russ (Shockey employee), 57

S

Saint Louis Naval Air Station, 39
Sampson Naval Training Station, 36

Sanka, 68
Saturday Evening Post, 16
Scalzo, Frank, 31
Scaz, Frankie, 17, 19, 67
Scully, Vin, 74
Sears, Roebuck and Company, 54
Sheft, Wally, 70
Shelly, Josh, 80
Sherman, Paul, 70
Shlank, Colgan, 61, 82
Sinclair, Upton, 16
Spielberg, Steven, 81
Steeplechase Park, 12
Steinbeck, John, 16
Stenchever's Shoes, 56
Suburban Propane Gas Company, 50–51
Suburban Propane News, 50

T

Tang, 68, 81
Technique for Producing Ideas, A (Young), 42
Texaco, 33, 75
This Is My God (Wouk), 35
Tirza (circus performer), 13
Tom Swift series, 16
Truth About Golf and Other Lies, The (Hackett), 74
TV commercials, 55, 76, 79

U

USS *Hector AR7*, 40
USS *Houston*, 40

V

Volkswagen, 43

W

Warner Bros., 77, 81
Waxmans, 11
Weiner, Walter, 57, 59
Whippany, New Jersey, 50
Williams, Ted, 19, 36
Wilson, Don, 67
Winters, Jonathan, 74
Winthrop's Vacuum Cleaners, 56
Woman's Home Companion, 16
wood shedding, 62–63
Woodward and Lothrop, 52
Work, Bob, 59, 62
World War II, 32–33, 39–40
Wouk, Herman
　This Is My God, 35

Y

Young, James Webb
　A Technique for Producing Ideas, 42
Y&R (Young & Rubicam), 58–59, 65, 69

Z

Zeyde (Alvin's grandfather), 21–23

www.ingramcontent.com/pod-product-compliance
Lightning Source LLC
Chambersburg PA
CBHW030859180526
45163CB00004B/1631